The Imagination of an Insurrection
At the Edge of History
Passages About Earth
Evil and World Order
Darkness and Scattered Light
The Time Falling Bodies Take to Light
Blue Jade from the Morning Star (Poetry)
Islands Out of Time (Fiction)
Pacific Shift
Gaia, A Way of Knowing (Editor)
Selected Poems, 1959–1989
Imaginary Landscape
Gaia Two: Emergence, The New Science of
Becoming (Editor)
Reimagination of the World (Co-author)

THE
AMERICAN REPLACEMENT
OF NATURE

WILLIAM IRWIN THOMPSON

THE
AMERICAN REPLACEMENT
OF NATURE

THE EVERYDAY ACTS
AND OUTRAGEOUS EVOLUTION
OF ECONOMIC LIFE

DOUBLEDAY
CURRENCY

NEW YORK   LONDON   TORONTO   SYDNEY   AUCKLAND

A Currency Book

PUBLISHED BY DOUBLEDAY

a division of Bantam Doubleday Dell Publishing Group, Inc.
666 Fifth Avenue, New York, New York 10103

CURRENCY and DOUBLEDAY are trademarks of Doubleday, a
division of Bantam Doubleday Dell Publishing Group, Inc.

Book design by Chris Welch

Library of Congress Cataloging-in-Publication Data

Thompson, William Irwin.
   The American replacement of nature by William Irwin
Thompson.—1st ed.
      p.   cm.
   "A Currency book"—
   1. United States—Popular culture—Philosophy.
   2. Culture—Philosophy. I. Title.
E169.12.T55   1991   91-3665
                                                       CIP

ISBN 0-385-42025-0

1   3   5   7   9   11   12   10   8   6   4   2

FOR JOHN CUTRER

Contents

Contents

THE
AMERICAN REPLACEMENT
OF NATURE

FAST FOREWORD

THE AMERICAN
REPLACEMENT OF NATURE

With ozone holes and greenhouse effects, earthquakes and tornadoes, statewide forest fires and floods, with exploding volcanoes in Hawaii and hurricanes of 200-mile-an-hour winds in the Virgin Islands, with glacial winters in the Midwest followed by summer droughts where not a zepher stirs nor a drop falls, you would think that Americans would be ready to call off the fight with nature; but, in fact, that explosive wildness is part of the climactic event: like a rocket that has all hell breaking loose in one direction so that a tiny nose cone can move in the other, a few technologists in the United States are determined to force their way out and surround nature with American culture. The very drama of nature lashing out against man, like the choreographed attacks in American televised wrestling, only serves to heighten the cinematic moment when the Hulk awakens from his feinted daze, sees the savage mass hurtling through the air toward him, rises, and deflects all the fury of the attack back on the rough beast to flatten him on the mat.

Mankind, and we are talking about *man-kind* here, has been waiting too long for this match, and whatever the New Age sissies in California may say about going back to a worship of the Goddess, a Riane Eisler partnership of compliant men with commanding women, and a life of quiet harmony nuzzled up against the bosom of nature, real Americans will have no truck with any of that. Just tune in to your Eurosport channel and watch those monster truck races in which the apotheosis of the Western pickup grinds down all those suburban family sedans and yuppie-mother–driven Volvo station wagons, and you'll see where it's really at. America is at it with a vengeance, and what *It* is, is Nature.

Travel agents in Europe report that more Europeans are traveling to America than ever before, and that tourism is fast becoming the United States' largest industry, but I can tell from conversations with my good Swiss neighbors that they really don't know what they are headed for in Orlando, Atlanta, and L.A. They have dutifully read all the guidebooks, for Europeans still do read books, and they do seem to like to approach a problem philosophically before they jump in to experience it—which is just about as far away from American culture as you can get.

America is not really an intellectual society, and so it has managed for two centuries to remain an ever teenage culture, and here Hollywood has helped keep up appearances with its display of macho technology and soft,

soap-opera feminine, relationship-oriented
sentimentality. Youth culture prefers fun to
angst and feeling good to feeling bad, so
American culture processors stick to making
special-effects films like *Back to the Future III*
for the boys, and relationboat soggies like
Steel Magnolias or *Stanley & Iris* for the girls.
Picture a teenage couple cruising in a con-
vertible and you have implicit in that youthful
moment under the sun a vision of destiny.
The boy grows up to become President Bush
in his speedboat, and the girl grows up
to become Mrs. Bush, with her lovely strand
of pearls; they don't grow up to become
European-type statesmen and -women or
artists.

Don't be fooled by intellectual spots like
Berkeley in California and Cambridge in
Massachusetts, for these are hothouses full of
rare and exotic European flowers; there, and
only there, you can hear talk of Heidegger or
Habermas, Foucault or Derrida, but just step
outside these tenured greenhouses to see what
the Texan capitalist climate is really like.
Sports stadiums, business schools, engineering labs, medical clinics (meaning biomedical
engineering labs): this is what your real
American university is like. It's a perilous life
being an intellectual in America, for anybody
can throw a rock through the greenhouse
glass or pull the plug, which is connected on
the outside to public sources of power.

For a brief interlude, after an unusually
virulent period of anti-intellectuality under

▼

Senator McCarthy, America, through JFK, flirted with European science and culture. Mrs. Kennedy spoke French and Spanish and even read Proust, which was awesome, but Reagan, Bush, and Quayle have pulled the country back onto its feet. Bush likes to hunt and fish; Gorbachev likes to read and have dialectical pillow talk with his philosophical wife, so you can be sure that Bush and Gorbachev didn't exactly fish and cut bait at their American summit in Camp David. Gorbachev asked to have lunch at the Soviet Embassy in Washington with the leaders of the American intelligentsia, and so Jane Fonda, Isaac Asimov, Ray Bradbury, and John Naisbitt were invited to represent the culture, which they did. Since Gorbachev had already spoken out against the threat of mass culture and entertainment in the European House, perhaps the Russian Ambassador was trying to reinforce his leader's vision that America was some kind of kid messing up the European Home with all that litter of Coca-Cola cans, McDonald's boxes, rock music albums, and Sylvester Stallone movies on the VCR. Clearly, getting the U.S. and the U.S.S.R. together isn't going to be easy when you consider that the attention span of a Russian is as long as one of their winters, and that you couldn't get an American to sit still through even one of those long panning shots in a Tarkovsky Russian film saga.

Still, Europeans shouldn't let the fact that Americans don't like Europe get in the way of their visiting America. If Americans would rather tour a fake Europe at EPCOT Center in Disney World, you have to understand that there they can go to "foreign" restaurants, but still speak English, and they can avoid the terrorists and thieves that abound in the frightful confusion of alien cultures in the real thing. Americans can skip Europe to go to EPCOT, but if Europeans try to skip America, they are missing out on what the future has in store for them in the American replacement of nature.

If America doesn't care much for antique, civilized European culture, you can imagine how it feels about old Stone Age Nature. Americans don't like Europe simply because it is too pretentious, intellectual, and infested with too damn many languages; but its dislike of Europe is greatly exceeded by its distaste for nature. Whereas men all around the world like to play football (soccer) practically in their underwear—T-shirts and boxer shorts —their splendor on the grass is primitive indeed when compared to American athletes encased in their space suits, charging with cleated foot on the eternal green of AstroTurf. In truth, America is extremely uncomfortable with nature; hence its culturally sophisticated preference for the fake and nonnatural, from Cheez Whiz sprayed out of an aerosol can onto a Styrofoam potatoed chip, to Cool Whip smoothing out the absence of taste in those attractively red, genetically engineered monster strawberries. Any peasant with a dumb cow can make whipped cream, but it takes a chemical factory to make Cool Whip. It is the technological process and not the natural product that is important, and if it tastes bad, well, that's beside the point, for what that point is aimed at, is the escape from nature. In America, even the food is a moon shot, a fast-food rocket aimed away from Earth.

Sure, Americans do like to hunt and fish, but not to commune with nature, rather to knock the old bitch around to show her who's boss. They leave the beer cans around in the wilderness just the way a dog pees on a tree: it shows they got there before you did. Same goes for pitching the tires in the creek, or parking the dead pickup truck in the weeds on the front yard, or leaving the old fridge on the porch. Seeing the water bubbling over the tires, or watching the weeds coming up through the floorboards: that's real harmony of man and nature. A few elitist snobs in the cities may be Sierra Club types, but they're really hypocrites, for they shove their trash out of sight. Country folks like to live with their trash, and that's probably the wave of the future too, as we run out of places to throw things away. And though people in the city like to call country folk "poor white trash," the truth is that in the United States, their kids go to college too, but they don't major in English or ecology; they major in engineering. Technology for them is another form of hunting or fishing; it's a way of getting back at nature. Whether it's raising the

6

flag on the moon, or leaving some high-tech trash out in space, it shows they got there before you did.

In Europe, you do philosophy by performing discourse on another guy's text, and so Derrida will go over Heidegger, and Habermas will extend Marx's corpus; but in America you could never get away with kinky stuff like that, for you have to generate philosophy from real things—like computers or television. You need to look at *Omni* magazine to get a feel for this new kind of mail-order, *Popular Mechanics* science of mind. It's full of articles about meditation helmets and downloading the soul into computers so that when your body wears out you can live forever. What is completely missing in Europe is precisely what you will find in America: namely, an electronic *Umwelt* in which history is replaced with movies, education is replaced with entertainment, and nature is replaced with technology. This peculiar wedding of low kitsch and high tech generates a posthistoric world that no European literary intellectual can quite fathom. Although Jean Baudrillard and Umberto Eco in their travel essays are fascinated by America's hyperreality, they always try to appropriate it as exotic ethnographic material for European discourse. They are more like moths drawn to a flame than swallows demonstrating the possibilities of air for imaginative flight. North American writers, such as Thomas Pynchon in his new novel *Vineland,* by con-

7

trast, perform the culture in the process of describing it: television shows and their fictional characters become milestones of artificial history—markers of time and space that tell the lost electronic consumer of the media where he parked his identity before his most recent purchase on reality.

As we move toward the Europe of 1992, our imagination over here is taken up with dreams of a culturally renascent Berlin, Prague, or Budapest, and we look to intellectual statesmen like Václav Havel to restore the culturally vibrant cities that we once knew in the Vienna of Wittgenstein or the Paris of Sartre. But these are old visions of ancient days, so perhaps it is not all that surprising that hypercompetitive America is not in the slightest degree interested in competing in this particular antiquarian exercise. In fact, America seems to be hitting the accelerator in the passing lane as it swings out to pass Europe and Japan and races into a culture that isn't really anything that you would want to call a culture, that is, by historical standards: but these standards are precisely what the Americans are passing by. In its shift from education to entertainment, from an industrial economy of commerce to an informational economy of commercials, America is getting it on with the unquestioning zest of a presidential campaign.

Judging by the banality of the last presidential campaign, you can begin to suspect that the U.S.A. is more than willing to accept an intellectual dark age as the necessary transition from a European and literate culture to a planetary and electronic one. Who knows, maybe evolution is on America's side, for those who do remember history can recall that there was a dark age in the transition from the oral culture of Homer to the literate culture of Aeschylus, so maybe Europe is going to be left behind as it hangs on to its civilized idea of what culture is all about. Evolution seems to work through the punctuated equilibrium of fits and starts, and big losses by the dinosaurs seem to precede big gains by the mammals. When life evolved from inanimate matter, molecules showed up inside cells. When mind evolved from life, cells showed up inside brains. If this new technological evolution has its way with us, minds may just end up inside it as animal organs are replaced by electronic lattices.

As an American living in Europe, I would like to recommend to my tourist neighbors some absolute musts in experiencing the North American replacement of nature. First is Orlando in the East, with its Disney World, EPCOT Center, and Disney-MGM Studios theme park, and last is the West Edmonton Mall in Alberta. West Edmonton Mall is the largest shopping mall in the world and has within it its own theme park, so it represents the ultimate stage in a cultural process that was initiated by London's Crystal Palace, confirmed by Milan's Galleria, consecrated by Los Angeles's Disneyland, and canonized by the West Edmonton

▼

Mall itself. It is no exaggeration to say that the historic European city, with its parliaments and cathedrals framing the plaza, has now been replaced by the shopping mall as the new articulation of civic space. In the historical era, monumental art, with its great buildings and its heroes on horseback, impressed the citizen with civilization; but now in our posthistoric condition, history is not a text, but a quote from old movies in a theme-park ride, or a commercial *for* CNN *on* CNN in which old news becomes a music video for passing time. In this shift from monumental art in space to cinematic entertainment in time, a dutiful life of personal sacrifice modeled after the guy up on the horse is replaced by participation in fantasies in which the intellect, and not the body, is offered up.

In a traditional society, the civic space is framed by Church and State—Westminster Abbey and the Houses of Parliament. In the Church there are two bodies—clergy and laity—and in the Parliament there are two houses—Lords and Commons, or Senate and House of Representatives. Archetypally, the upper house expresses the slower and more mature outlook of wisdom and reflection— the accumulated knowledge of civilization and the ages; while the lower house expresses the shortsighted concerns of the single issue and the pressing needs of the moment. In the posthistorical society of the state of Entertainment, this balance is reflected in reporters

▼

and commentators. The reporter is the commoner's voice describing events in the immediacy of action, live from Baghdad; the commentator is the retired general or academic providing the lordly wisdom of the past in interpreting the images that irradiate our unsuspecting minds.

It is only natural that in this artificial world, one shifts from an enduring way of life to transitional lifestyles. The airport–shopping mall–theme park city becomes the new body politic, the civic space of temporary incarnations, those momentary purchases on reality in which the past is redeemed by the future in the symbolic act of charging time. The credit card is the real passport of our multinational corporate era—the magnetized strip that shows us for what we really are underneath our clothes, and allows us to pass through security checks at airports and hotels and across innumerable boundaries of the quaint boutique nation-states of EPCOT and the world about it.

It is not a long way from Orlando to Atlanta, and a trip to Orlando is the right introduction to the new Atlanta of the CNN Center and the 1996 world Olympics. In the architecture of the Orlando airport, Disney World, EPCOT, the CNN Center, and the West Edmonton Mall, one experiences monumentality not as an expression of a cosmology or a historical text—be it the Gospels or the Magna Carta—but as a movie-set construction or a department store window that calls forth a desire to perform. Here you are not dwelling in a place, you are on location in a movie that is all about you. Spectacle becomes as important for the disliterate multitudes of electronic society as it was for the illiterate populace of the Middle Ages. Precisely because entertainment has now replaced education as the basic process of socialization, "Entertainment News" is given on CNN along with the day's activities in politics and economics, because in this new media society, entertainment is both politics and economics.

The genius of American global management comes from oversimplification and a brazen willingness to miniaturize the immense. The CNN Center in Atlanta is a rendering of Teilhard de Chardin's noosphere; it is a planetary lattice of satellites in which nonstop 24-hours-a-day news gives us the experience of time under control—history under new American management. As a miniaturization of the noosphere, the CNN Center in Atlanta is the perfect introduction to the miniaturization of the planetary biosphere in Biosphere II near Tucson, Arizona. Since the idea of the historic city and the idea of the posthistoric theme park have both been contained in the West Edmonton Mall, it is not surprising that America has responded to the competition from its cowboy Albertan neighbor to the north in a good old Texan fashion of doing it bigger and better by building a container, not just for a city, but for an entire biosphere. In funding Biosphere II, the Bass brothers of Texas have shown just where America's heart really is in this global competition. Forget about all the glass of the Crystal Palace or the Galleria, we're talking about American evolutionary management under there. And if it just so happens that pollution and deforestation destroy all the medicinal plants that the multinational pharmaceutical corporations need for their wonder drugs, well then Biosphere II might just turn out to be a good investment: not a rehearsal for some sci-fi space colony on Mars, but a crossing of a nineteenth-century French art museum with a twentieth-century Swiss electronic bank, a late-capitalist institution to corner the market on life and store the genetic capital for a troubled, cyberpunk world.

Last stop is any Virtual Reality lab around San Francisco or Seattle. At the edge of nature in the farthest West of America, it is no accident that the final act in the American replacement of nature should be the replacement of the body's incarnation in real time with the mind's reincarnation into Virtual Reality. In these Virtual Reality laboratories of the West Coast, a new electronic space suit has been invented that allows individuals to put on the TV set to become their own show. Indeed, this electronic condom comes not a moment too soon, for as so many HIV positive people have begun to lie and become careless again, the only "safe sex" in the future will be in the excitement of touching one

another's projections in the communion of
Virtual Realities. The miniature TV sets that
are mounted as goggles over the eyes that
allow this transformation of artistic space into
cyberspace give the appearance of being a
new Neanderthal, supraorbital ridge, an evolution of the hominid forehead in which the
Self becomes the theater itself. Gone are pro-
scenium arch and theatrical stage separating
observer and actor; on hand is the NASA
glove that enables you to point your finger
and fly beyond the limits of the painter's can-
vas and the director's screen.

McLuhan said that every media extension
of man is a biological amputation, that those
who have cars don't walk to the store. Rock
music brought with it deafness in middle age
for its youth culture aficionados, so perhaps
these goggles with their electromagnetic
fields of noise may cause cataracts and glau-
coma for hackers in their thirties. But not to
worry, for the American commitment to
technology is too faithful to seek divorce on
the basis of merely one organic infidelity.
Trust Silicon Valley to come up with a new
California therapy that will go beyond the
peripheral sensory system to Dr. José Del-
gado's direct implants in the brain, ones that
do not require the act of having to "see" an
"outside" world, but whose electric stimu-
lation of the pleasure centers can make or-
gasm seem like a genital sneeze. The brain
will be so hot-wired that one will never have
to move; one could, like the old Philco TV

ads of the fifties, have one's "works in a drawer." With the breath of the body almost suspended, we are laid asleep in body to become a living soul, was what the poet Wordsworth said, but he had something else in mind, and anyway that was Europe and a long time ago, but this is Dan Quayle's Spaceship America, with the pilgrim soul on file in its mortuary drawer, making the voyage to Mars away from Earth's dragging gravity and evolution's sloppy flesh.

PLAY

DISNEY'S WORLD:
THE AMERICAN
REPLACEMENT OF CULTURE

Like a fossil inside a rock that tells the story of evolution, there is a movie theater immediately to the right as you come into Disney World; it is the old-time movie theater of Main Street, U.S.A., and there in this theater, the life of Disney is shared with the public. Walt explains how Disneyland was a response to his aesthetic revulsion at the sordid underside of life that was so characteristic of the old amusement park, and how, as the father of a family living in Southern California, there was not much to do of a Sunday besides driving those vast distances to stop at various roadside attractions, snake farms, and jelly stands with curios. With television in the home, entertainment outside it had to be something more than the seamy carnival and freak show or the small-town circus. In his unconscious and completely unintellectual exercise of a Hegelian *Aufheben,* Disney's intuitive genius led him to lift up the movie set and cross it with the amusement park to allow each person to become star of his or her own movie by giving access, not to the end product of a movie set in a film, but to the process itself. The movie set became the carnival ride, a literal *carnevale,* a farewell to flesh in a new vehicle, a new subtle body of consciousness with which to envelop the old flesh of matter. As religion was becoming sunlit and suburban and the terrors of mystical experiences were fading away in the drive-in, top-down churches of Southern California, Disney transformed ancient and mythic frightful rites of initiation into the modern entertainment of frightful rides.

The central experience of a ride in a theme park is empowerment of the body through surrender to the vehicle, and empowerment of consciousness through the distancing of evil. In a frightful ride, you may scream in the delight of a safe terror, and you can confront evil in the way that the soul in death might look back at the distant world of the ego in its former life. In Disney World's Pirates of the Caribbean, the experience is one in which evil is distanced, miniaturized, and made light of. "Hi ho, hi ho, it's off to rape we go" could almost be the song of the pirates, as we slide in our barques past scenes of burning ports, seized women, and loaded plunder. Of course, as with all levels of social technology, from hunting to space travel, there is a shadow side to Disney's distancing of evil. Just as the Mesolithic bow and arrow of the hunt became the Neolithic weapon of battle, so Disney's technique for distancing evil can become the technique for training fighter pilots in their vehicles. There now exists an electronic helmet for jet pilots that transforms the physical terrain ahead into an abstract video map; radar warns the pilot of hidden rockets, fighters, or artillery, so that he can press the button in time to eliminate the threats. The video map becomes a video game. But the shadow also is shadowed, for when war becomes so fast that no human jet-fighter pilot can possibly respond in time, war can no longer be played by humans in time; it either has to be deferred to robots and artificial intelligence or eliminated entirely when one realizes that one's enemy out there is actually a projection of one's self in here.

As secular camouflage for a civic religion, Disneyism involves two basic moves in its strategy of appealing to the unconscious. The first shift is to move from traditional emphases on transcendence of the physical through sexual negation in celibacy to a more immanent passage into the psychic in the context of the family as the basic group sharing in the fantasy. No longer do we have the case of the yogi in retreat from women, alone in his cave in the trance of *samadhi;* and no longer do we have the case of the celibate nun, a St. Teresa being stabbed with an angelic arrow in her heart that sends her into cosmic ecstasy: this case is a car filled with Dad, Mom, and the kids, screaming in terror and delight as they drop in the darkness of the noisy hell of the Space Mountain ride, or drift in Bardo past the evils of the Haunted Mansion.

Since Disneyland and Disney World are set up to be experienced by the family, I would like to approach them on their own terms, as both son and father experiencing Disneyism in the intended familial context over the span of a generation.

I must have been four or five when my mother took me to see *Fantasia* in Chicago. To go from the family space to this vast darkness that yet was a communal space shared with others, well, there was simply nothing like it except Mass on Sunday; but I didn't like going to Mass, because Father Quinn was always shouting at us from the pulpit that the congregation was not giving enough money to the Church. The church was a cold and dark place, and all around were images of people being tortured, and in the very center there was this twisted corpse of Jesus on the cross. I was told that he had to be nailed to the cross because we had sinned, and so now we owed it to him to accept our suffering in life and give money to the Church. I did not like Father Quinn, but I had to kneel below him in the pew. But my father never knelt, and when I asked my mother why Dad never knelt, she said it was because he was a Protestant and didn't have to. Lucky him, I thought, and wondered why I wasn't a Protestant.

It was a theater of suffering and torture when my mother took me to church, but when she took me to my first movie, it was a true religious experience. With its enormous darkness and a two-story-high screen, with the music clearer and stronger than anything I had ever heard from the Gothic wooden box of our radio, with the delightfully affectionate mouse, a creature who was as small and vulnerable as I was, and then with that whole cosmology of planetary evolution that unrolled before me to the music of Stravinsky, the movie theater became for me a ritual of initiation, the Paleolithic cave of Lascaux and the ancient Greek mysteries of Eleusis in one. I became that soul again approaching the planet Earth to accept a human incarnation; it wasn't a metaphor, it was a memory. This racial memory of vast cosmic spaces meant far more to me than the mangled Christ on the altar next to the screaming Father Quinn in the pulpit. Here was the explanation of who I was, where I came from, and where I was going. In watching the evolution of the planet, the march of the dinosaurs, and the progression of all the old mentalities of animism, with elves and fairies, nymphs, and sorcerers, I was being instructed in the mysteries of the evolution of consciousness, not Germanically by Jean Gebser, but cinematically by Walt Disney, and I was having my own consciousness shifted from animism to materialism to the new informationalism of the medium of film.

When the war ended in 1945, like so many midwesterners, my family moved to Los Angeles. I saw the red Pacific Electric city trains dismantled and replaced by automotive free-

21

ways, saw the orange groves bulldozed into
subdivisions, and saw the shopping malls and
campus universities like U.C. Irvine grow
into one another. And when I was in high
school, in the era now so continuously re-
quoted in the imagery of fin-tailed Bel Air
Chevies and Cadillac Eldorados, in those fifties when America was at the peak of its
world hegemony, at the time of the creation
of Disneyland, I was in L.A. Considering that
construction on Disneyland had started on
my sixteenth birthday in 1954, I should have
been on hand for its opening a year and a day
later, but I would not know how to appreciate
the fifties in Southern California until the
extraordinary summer of 1967 when the
transformation of consciousness through
California had become a national enterprise.

The truth is that I was an intellectual snob
and was disgusted with all the fuss about Disneyland that was being made by my teachers
and administrators at Los Angeles High. We
were supposed to be a school, not an entertainment industry, and so I was ashamed at
all the interest being shown by people who,
I thought, should be above all that. As an
intellectual in the McCarthy era, I was a mis-
fit. I hated Elvis Presley, and the records I
bought were not red 45s with big holes, but
Columbia Masterworks recordings of the
Budapest String Quartet playing Beethoven
on Stradivarius instruments in the Library of
Congress. I read James Joyce's *A Portrait of
the Artist as a Young Man* and dreamed of liv-

ing in Europe. Here I was living in the most important world city for the cultural transformation of industrial into postindustrial society, and all I wanted was to be in some "real" place like Cole Porter's New York of the thirties, T. S. Eliot's London of the twenties, or Joyce's Dublin of the turn of the century. I would have nothing to do with Disneyland until 1967, when I myself was a parent of a five-year-old and had returned from living in Dublin to Los Angeles to work on my book *At the Edge of History*.

So, like a dutiful father, I took my son to Disneyland, and was amazed at how much it had to tell me about the course on the history of the city I was then teaching at M.I.T. What *Fantasia* was for me at five, Disneyland was to become for my five-year-old son. We were in Captain Nemo's submarine in Tomorrowland, staring out the portal at the monsters of the deep. Suddenly a shark lunged at our window, and Evan grabbed my hand in terror. I laughed and tried to calm his anxieties by saying, "Relax, it's not real." We moved on through the deep, but there was something all too real about this underwater world for Evan, and he seemed deeply disturbed. When the giant squid attacked us, he again screamed in fear, and once again I tried to calm his anxieties by saying, "Relax, it's not real." But by classing so vibrant an experience as unreal, I had unwittingly awakened a deeper ontological anxiety by bracketing reality itself, and the five-year-old phenomenologist looked up at me, comparing our physical reality with the psychic reality on the other side of the portal, and said, "Dad, are we real?" I laughed in amazement and delight at his philosophical precosity, and answered, "Well, there are some mystics who would say, 'Not really.' " If *Fantasia* imprinted me for life with a fascination for myth and cosmogony, then so did the submarine ride imprint Evan, for he grew up to become a philosopher and cognitive scientist, writing books on theories of perception.[1]

So the snob in me had to repent and accept the facts of life that Disneyland did work as intended. It was family fun and part of the way of life of Los Angeles. But Disney World in Florida is something else, a world apart, a new political culture. What is spontaneous, playful, and harmless kitsch in Disneyland becomes more planned, more controlled, and more iconically manipulative at Disney World. You can spend a day at Disneyland, and then go home; but at Disney World, you are there for the duration, and there is no escape from the unending programs of indoctrination. Disneyism, of course, like any other religion has its movement from charisma to routine. When the founding visionary dies, the managers and functionaries of the Church take over. There is a sense of innocent fun at Disneyland, and whatever corporate giantism hovers about Tomorrowland can be accepted as the commercial that interrupts the program but pays for it. How-

ever, at Disney World and especially at EP-
COT, the commercial becomes the entire
program.

EPCOT means Experimental Prototype
Community of Tomorrow, but the porters
at Disney World's Contemporary Resort say
that it stands for "Every Person Comes Out
Tired." They come out tired because every
giantesque corporate pavilion, from Exxon
to General Motors, seems to be saying to the
little guy, "Me Tarzan, you Jane." You come
out tired, because EPCOT is not fun; it's serious business, and every sound-bite and image you experience is programmed. Your
emotional responses are as manipulated as
they would be in a commercial for a Presidential campaign. Mussolini's Italian fascist
architects and Hitler's Nürnberg rally media
geniuses—Speer and Riefenstahl—seem to
have reincarnated among us as Disney's "Imagineers" celebrating American power in a
manner in which our old enemies become
born-again patriots. The magic of Disney's
"Magic Kingdom" of the fifties is gone, and
the electropop machinations of the eighties
and nineties, the age of Reagan, Casey,
North, Bush, and Quayle, are up front and
center stage. Small wonder that Jim and
Tammy Bakker tried to imitate Disney's genius and build their own fundamentalist
Christian theme park, and small wonder that
the television evangelists come on like rhine-
stone cowboys, for Disney World is the
Lourdes of the Sunbelt, the place of miracles

25

and the patriotic apotheosis of the common man.

Your journey to EPCOT starts with a ride on the monorail. And as you stand in line to board, you do not behave as you might on a subway platform in New York or Tokyo. As the executives of the Disney corporation have said in *Time:* "Think of Disney World as a small city with a crime rate of zero." Walt Disney's way of achieving this good behavior in the fifties was by making the place, unlike an ordinary amusement park, immaculately clean, swept and serviced by polite and wholesome young people working their way through college, and by having an entrance fee high enough to keep the riffraff out. The Imagineers of today have gone on to more sophisticated levels of crowd management by understanding the subliminal use of sound. As you stand in a long line to wait for the monorail, you hear the song on the piped-in Muzak, "When You Wish Upon a Star." Even if you do not listen, you remember the *Pinocchio* film of your childhood and the lovable Jimminy Cricket, and you are inclined to sense that something wonderful is about to happen to you as you prepare to enter "The Magic Kingdom."

The scary thing about this manipulation of the body politic through sound is that it really does work. People do behave; they are both patient and polite. As the philosopher of the evolution of consciousness Jean Gebser recognized as he wandered in Europe as a refugee

from the fascism of Hitler's Germany and
Franco's Spain: the emphasis on sight and linear perspective is a characteristic of the Mental era of development that came in with the
Italian Renaissance; but the older levels of
consciousness, the Mythic and the Magical,
were aural worlds in which sounds wove people into the fabric of life.[2] The modern age
of the individual is the era of the individual
at the pointed end of a pyramidal field of
vision created by perspective. The modern
individual, your educated middle-class patri-
arch, is the reader, alone in his book-lined
study trying to understand the world through
the texts of civilization. This is the world of
Marshall McLuhan's Gutenberg Galaxy and
Jean Gebser's Mental structure. Both Mc-
Luhan in Toronto and Gebser in Bern recognized that modernism was over and that
we were moving into a new structure of consciousness. The age of the literate individual
with his mind at work in his library and his
representative at work in his parliament is
over, and the sound of the passing of this era
is noise itself. Noise is the solvent of Renaissance individuality; it is the sound that does
not grant the individual the space or solitude
for wise and informed reflection. Whether
for a teenager in a discotheque, a yuppie in
a noisy restaurant, or a middle-aged matron
in a shopping mall, silence is not felt to be
a stimulating occasion for reflection; it is
a frightening and negative thing, an aural
darkness.

27

No one understands this better than Disney's Imagineers. In the elevators and the monorails, what you hear is not a random Muzak of washed-out Beatles songs, but carefully selected tunes from your childhood memories of Disney movies. History is not a text, and so recollection becomes the re-gathering of images and sounds, of Jimminy Cricket or Tinker Bell.

When you enter EPCOT, you encounter Bucky Fuller's geodesic sphere, Spaceship Earth; it is a Yankee engineer's vision of the planet as a machine designed for motion in space. With your old identity parked outside in the lot, you pass on from being a paid worker in industrial society to becoming a paying consumer in the postindustrial world of the city as shopping mall. As you emerge from the sphere of Spaceship Earth, you extend your spatial horizons to take in the majestic architecture of General Motors' World of Motion and Exxon's Universe of Energy, and as you hear majestic, David Lean–sounding movie themes coming up from the speakers hidden in the marigolds, you feel that some wonderful experience is about to sweep you off your feet.

Indeed, in General Motors' World of Motion the individual *is* lifted off his feet, but in that ride in which the speakers celebrate the freedom of motion, he is not allowed to move but is strapped down, not to be released until the end when he is set before the showroom that contains General Motors' newest models on display for inspection and admiration. Similarly, in Exxon's Universe of Energy, the kids are taken in by a ride past the dinosaurs of the past, just as the parents are taken for a ride with films of nuclear reactors that, we are told, provide much of Chicago's needed energy. What was only toyed with in General Electric's Carousel of Progress at the old Disneyland is now a full-scale celebration of corporate America, a commercial from which there is no escape, for this is indeed the prototype community in which entertainment and not education molds the voter of tomorrow.

Although EPCOT proclaims itself to be the community of tomorrow; it is certainly the *noetic* polity of today. Whereas a *sanguinal* polity is a tribal one in which identity is based on relationship through blood, on being, for example, the children of Abraham, and a *territorial* polity is one in which identity is based on land defined by boundaries, a noetic polity is based upon states of consciousness. The Catholic Church, and then modern science, were the first noetic polities, but what is now emerging is a new planetary noetic polity that is a neo-medieval synthesis of both, in that it is as hierarchical as the Church and as technologically based as modern science. In our contemporary cultural formations, such as global electronic banking, pop music, and Disney World, you can begin to make out the shape of things to come.

The cultural unconscious of EPCOT is

more interesting than its conscious propaganda, for as a physical shape it is definitely
not futuristic, but is most definitely the old
automobile city of the Southern California
1950s. Everyone who works there lives far
away in the cheaper housing of distant bed-
room communities, or worse, the trailer
camp settlements of the real working class.
And when you drive to work, you don't enter
through Bucky Fuller's sphere, but by a service road behind all the movie sets of the
pavilions in the theme park. If you enter EP-
COT from the back of the movie set, you are
not *Homo ludens* (Man the player), but a
worker in the old industrial culture of *Homo
faber* (Man the maker). In the service and
trucking zone behind the shopping mall, you
see no fountains, but simply parked cars,
Dempsey Dumpsters, and boxy, warehouse
architecture. It's about as exciting and as
truthful as seeing a presidential candidate
without his photo-op smile.

30

Drama presented in the open space of the
Greek theater was a popular art form that
brought the community together in the face-
to-face manner that contributed to the open
space of direct democracy in the Greek polis.
In the shift from direct democracy to repre-
sentational democracy, the printed book became an embodiment of thought for the
physically absent author; and so the popular
art form of the printed book and the pamphlet
re-presented ideas and contributed to the
public space of the political philosophies of

the Enlightenment. Television, however, now brings forth this new kind of public space, and it calls into being this new world, not of the educated citizenry in a republic, but of the electropeasantry in the state of Entertainment. Recall how people stopped singing in pubs when they brought in the TV set, and you will appreciate the new passivity in which people stop voting for their representatives as TV takes over the electoral campaigns. Kindergarten teachers tell me that children no longer sing spontaneously, for they know that songs are what the famous sing on MTV. They hope, someday, to grow up to become Pepsi's Madonna, but in the meantime the only songs for which they know the words are commercials.

It is not all that far from a televised song to a televised election. The cultural implications of EPCOT are that this noncommunity is a real polity, one that actually performs the transition from plutocracy to mediocracy— a society of the mediocre bonded together by the entertainment media. This new polity is one in which "democracy" becomes an artifact, an antique culture in quotes within a new society, not one of *representation* in a literate republic, but of fantasy *participation* in the electronic state. The citizen votes for someone who expresses his or her philosophy and represents it in Congress; the electropeasant votes for someone he or she likes; it is not a question of mental reflection but magical participation: Bush runs for President fig-

31

ured against a gigantic American flag and Dukakis puts on a helmet and takes a ride in a tank. The technicians who demand that these photo opportunities be produced for public consumption are members of the same profession that created The American Adventure at EPCOT.

Outside this pavilion, by the shore of the artificial lagoon, an African ensemble performs tribal music and dance, but a few yards away, closer to the entrance, a Dixieland band loudly drowns them out. America has never been very good at hearing the Third World, and although it enjoys ethnicity in restaurants, it tends to transform disturbingly complex black jazz into fun-loving white Dixieland music. Inside the pavilion this system of taming the wild is carried further as that dirty old man Benjamin Franklin and that sarcastic old bastard Mark Twain are turned into ushers for a ritual in the civic religion of Disneyism. Franklin and Twain introduce us to another movie-set experience of the spatialization of time as all the presidents of American history are brought to life on stage in an Audio-Animatronics display in the Hall of Presidents. The only other place in which they all could be together is heaven, so it is possible that some people do get a little disoriented in the dark of the theater. With a vision of all the presidents before them, the stirring music of fife and drum just becomes too much for many people, and they begin to weep in seizures of patriotism.

Pay no mind to the Wizard of Oz behind the curtain, for every image and sound-bite is controlled by a bank of computers and a group of technicians that would make NASA proud—but that is no different from your average presidential campaign. There too a group of invisible technicians serves an equally invisible board of directors. What Disney prefigured, Reagan figured as he became the first entirely Audio-Animatronic President, a loveable creation that performed perfectly according to the programming of the technicians and the dictates of the board of directors. As to who serves on the board of directors of this America, I certainly have no way of knowing. Right-wing paranoids will tell you that it is the Rockefellers with their Trilateral Commission, but I doubt it, for that sounds much more like a projection of the right-wingers' own alienated way of working in secret paramilitary cells and survivalist colonies; the old rich of any society need no secret conspiracy, because the old-boy networks within the ruling institutions have all the power that is needed to run a Great Britain or a United States.

A presidential campaign, exactly like the Olympics, which also come every fourth year, is an electronic spectator sport; it is a spectacle for professionals who have trained themselves for this world of celebrity performances, of smiles, sound-bites without substance or controversy, and stirring images. In this world of emotional signaling, it is more important to protect the flag than civil liberties. The flag is not a symbol of a revolution fought to achieve civil liberties from kings and cardinals; it is a symbol, not of individuation, but of collectivization, of the electropeasant's bond to the body politic. If the flag is burned, then he or she is burned. Rational citizens, as children of the Enlightenment, will burn the flag to make a statement about constitutional rights, but electropeasants will ignite in rage at their own disfigurement.

The entertainment industry's reconstruction of American history in The American Adventure is, when all is said and done, a dutiful exercise. After all, if history is not a text any longer, then history for the state of Entertainment is motion-picture history. Memories are not of historical events, they are recollections of past movies. Recall that President Reagan wept on several occasions on recalling his old World War II days, and remember that he was not recalling his own experiences of historical events, such as Omaha Beach or Iwo Jima; he was remembering the old war movies he had seen or played in. If you can understand the sensibility of President Reagan, then you can enter into this new kind of political Virtual Reality to appreciate why the designers of MGM Studios theme park would try to recapture "major moments in motion-picture history," and why Cable News Network presents "The Hollywood Minute" and "This Week in

Show Biz." For the history-less people of this postliterate generation, it makes no sense to take them through The American Adventure, for these people have not read Benjamin Franklin or Mark Twain. But if you take them on the Indiana Jones ride in the Disney—MGM Studios theme park, now that is different, for the hat and the whip are icons, and the people will thrill to the joy of remembering the movie.

In the old rides in Disneyland, like Pirates of the Caribbean and Haunted Mansion, it was the distancing of evil that was the setting up of space; safe in one's barque one could glide by the scenes of the pirates burning the town and carrying off the women. In the new Disney-MGM Studios theme park near Disney World, the structure is the setting up of time as a manufactured horizon, a fake artifact of the past: not a personal past or a national history, but a memory of a movie you have seen. It used to be, "You've read the book, now thrill to the movie." Now it is, "You've seen the movie, now thrill to the ride." Lucas and Spielberg are men of my generation, of the fifties in L.A. As children of McLuhan's global village, they did not need to read McLuhan to understand that when a cliché is repeated, or used as a model for a new performance, the cliché becomes an archetype. So old World War II movies like *Air Force* become the model for *Star Wars*. When a cliché becomes an archetype, old movies become myths; they become horizons that add

35

the dimension of the past to the present. Since *Raiders of the Lost Ark* is a copy of a movie serial, which is a copy of a comic book, an illusionary depth to time, a manufactured tradition, is created in which copy copies copy. What is important is not that this is all fake, for the content is irrelevant; it is the horizonal structure of the experience that is important. And that structure is one of magnifying and extending time to provide for people doomed to the shallow present of an electronic-media society a substitute for a historical consciousness. You feel nostalgic for a past, and it doesn't matter if those tilted DC-3s and Bogey walking away with Claude Rains on the tarmac is not really your experiential past. After all, what is experience in an electronic society? The important thing is that those images are in your memory as images of the past, for that makes them part of your experience. It's all the same past for kids for whom Humphrey Bogart playing African sailor or Chicago gangster, or Charlton Heston playing Moses, God, or Michelangelo are all old folks back there in time with George Washington, the Beatles, Louis Armstrong, and Babe Ruth. If you grew up with fifty channels on your TV set, or Hypercard stacks in your personal computer, then the past is not a text that moves from left to right with everything dated in a linear fashion from B.C. to A.D.

For posthistoric Los Angeles, as Nathanael West pointed out long ago in his novel *The*

Day of the Locust, history becomes a movie set that spatializes time: on one studio lot you have Caesar and Cleopatra, while next to it the Sioux are defeating Custer. For the young raised on electronic media, there is no historical past, there is only an eternal present in which all time is going on now. The narrative through which you construct events into a world is not a narrative of personal history, but a pastiche of lifestyles. Lifestyles are expressed in costumes that are a patchwork of signs purchased in a boutique. Furniture for the young is not an artifact of a king, a Louis Quatorze, but a poster of a celebrity, a Coca-Cola wastepaper basket, a Mobil gas pump light, and a war-surplus inflatable life-raft bed. These signs, whether they are worn around as furniture or on as clothes, have a recognizable nostalgic feeling to them, but no real history. In the costume as lifestyle, you don't become your own movie, as you might have done in the generation of the Depression, you become your own music video; in the former you have an identity that unfolds its story, but in the latter you have a collage that flashes its momentary mood and passing style.

37

These children of *Sesame Street* and MTV will not grow up to become responsible citizens with a highly developed sense of civic duty, but they will express a highly magical sense of global participation in sound that allows the skin of their own bodies to become the vibrating tympanum of a new collective entity. In fact, this is precisely why the young like to have their music loud. If you go into a bar that is a "body shop" for the young, it is not a pub in which you can have a conversation; it is a space in which all the bodies are kneaded into shape by physically palpable, extremely loud noise. You don't go there to exchange ideas but to drum your edge, to feel the beat and the pulse in which you become part of the scene. Like motile spirochetes that billions of years ago attached themselves to large and sluggish cells in the evolution of bacteria, this new noisy critter made up out of people is a piece of "connectionist architecture" that is headed for forms of life we old folks can hardly imagine.

A person of my generation simply cannot stand to be in these spaces for even a few moments. Just as noise in public spaces takes away the silence necessary for mature and knowledgeable reflection, so does our entire invisible environment of electronic noise, from microwave to ELF (extremely low-frequency radiation from transmission cables, wires, and video display terminals), take away the biological autonomy of the etheric membrane of the individual. The ultimate development in this direction is not a ride in the dark in Disney's Pirates of the Caribbean but an immersion into cyberspace in which one's own etheric body is pirated by the electronic noise of a full body suit immersion into Virtual Reality.

The full body suit is a technological literalization of the esoteric subtle body, or etheric body, the *pranamayakosa* of Yoga and Tibetan Buddhism. This envelope of the subtle body is also the point of focus in Chinese acupuncture and in the martial arts such as kung fu. By interfering with its functioning and by appropriating it in a literalization that imitates but degrades its esoteric functioning, the individual is shifted away from the autonomy of its own membrane in its incarnation toward a collective incarnation. To understand this shift one has to read cyberpunk fiction or the works of Rudolf Steiner who predicted this state of cultural evolution and called it the emanation of Ahriman.[3] Unfortunately, this reference to Steiner will probably upset students of cognitive science, but they should ask themselves why practitioners of artificial life in software worlds often get the feeling that if there are worlds below them, then there could well be worlds above them, cognitive domains that exist in multidimensionality.[4]

William Gibson, the leading practitioner of cyberpunk science fiction and the writer who coined the term "cyberspace," is clearly fascinated with the nature of evil as the new landscape of electronic technology, and in his novel *Count Zero,* he has crossed voodoo with artificial intelligence. The cognitive scientist who is willing to take in voodoo should not be so quick to throw out Steiner, for thinkers as subtle and gifted as England's Owen Barfield, Germany's Joseph Beuys, and Ameri-

ca's Saul Bellow have been fascinated with
Steiner's philosophy. There *is* something to
it, and if one wishes to understand the new
electronic landscape that dematerializes our
old worldview, then one can learn from Steiner without fear of having to enroll in his
Anthroposophical movement.

Rudolf Steiner was an intellectual mystic
whose philosophical movement, through the
normal Weberian process of the routinization
of charisma, has now become a somewhat
rigid and humorless cult; therefore, one can
argue that if religion ends up in deception and
distances itself from the original vision, it
might be more true to the spirit to begin with
deception itself in the realms of art and entertainment in order to constellate a disguised
congregation sharing an unconscious cosmology. In his 1940 film *Fantasia*—which has
recently been rereleased in 1990 to celebrate
its fiftieth birthday—Disney reintroduced the
animistic cosmology in which the fairies and
elves embody the seasonal powers of nature.
By constellating a congregation through fun
and entertainment, Disney was also able to
use his films and his public following to amass
the capital needed to found his electronic polity of Disneyland and Disney World. Science-
fiction writers and computer-game hackers
have continued this evolutionary crossing of
preindustrial animism and postindustrial capitalism by reintroducing the world of sorcery
and the great battle between good and evil,
between black and white magic, into their

software. All these different types of minds have reintroduced animism because the conventional worldview of materialism is not subtle enough to deal with the complexities of a multidimensional universe in which domains interpenetrate and are infolded in one another in a non-euclidean manner. Vernor Vinge explained the fascination in his story "True Names," which, in 1979, was one of the first science-fiction ventures into cyberspace.

> Mr. Slippery had often speculated just how the simple notion of using high-resolution EEGs as input/output devices had caused the development of the "magical world" representation of data space. The Limey and Erythrina argued that sprites, reincarnation, spells, and castles were the natural tools here, more natural than the atomistic twentieth-century notions of data structures, programs, files, and communications protocols. It was, they argued, just more convenient for the mind to use the global ideas of magic as the tokens to manipulate this new environment.[5]

41

Ever since I saw *Fantasia* as a child of four or five, I have resisted Roman Catholicism and remained a Celtic animist at heart and have known from the trance states I experienced from listening to classical music that the conventional religious and materialistic worldview of my society was inadequate. Over the years the encounter with other phi-

losophies and esoteric schools of contempla-
tive practice, such as Yoga and Buddhism,
have given me ancient maps for the new
world I had entered as a child—not through
jacking into cyberspace on William Gibson's
laptop "Ono-Sendai," but through Bach,
Beethoven, and Stravinsky.

What the Buddhist discovers in meditation
is that there is no absolute, discrete, "self,"
but that there are infinite relations in all di-
rections that are instrumental in bringing
forth beings that pass together (compassion
= passing together) in concerts of time and
space. The enlightened being travels more
lightly than the heavy ego burdened with the
matter of his or her afflictions, and the enlightened being can easily offer its music in
concert with others to experience mystical
states of union with Buddhas and bodhisatt-
vas, angels and gods, or a vast and universal
form of Godhead beyond the personifications
of deities. The being that cannot open itself
to these multiple dimensions chooses not to
create its destiny, but to have its fate inflicted
upon it in the samsaric form of suffering and
evil. Notice how in our technological culture
we can enthusiastically embrace Gibson's cyberpunk visions of voodoo and evil far more
readily than we can Steiner's theosophical visions of angels and grace. In literature, dys-
topias are always far more compelling than
vapid clerical visions of heavenly virtue. Gibson's work is enthralling because he understands as a writer that evil is the annunciation

42

of a newly emerging level of societal organization.[6] But if one truly wishes to understand the landscape of electronic noise in which the individual etheric body is so assaulted that an individual soul can no longer incarnate in a human body, then one has to read Steiner. The *Mondo 2000* magazine enthusiasts and apologists for the new technology of neuroreceptor drugs and full body suit immersions into Virtual Reality will never discuss the side effects, so one needs Rudolf Steiner to balance the hype of the California snake-oil salesmen of drugs and computers.

In the sixties, LSD externalized the collective unconscious, the astral plane, albeit in a kitsch and degraded form. This appropriation of the astral plane into the public space is now being followed up by the appropriation of the etheric plane. As cyberdelic drugs combine with the effects of the invisible environment of drugs in foods and the polluted biosphere, the cumulative effect will be to erode organic autonomy and lower fertility rates (this has already begun to happen); and this will stimulate medibusiness to compete with agribusiness. Just as America appropriated the family farm into feedlots and factories, so will it appropriate the family into the laboratory. Thus the appropriation of the astral body in the sixties through LSD, and the appropriation of the etheric body in the nineties, will pave the way for the final act of the appropriation of the physical body around the turn of the century. Thus America, the land of rugged individualism will become the land of ragged individuals, first economically, and then physiologically. Through genetic engineering, in vitro insemination, and reproductive technologies yet to come, the individual will be so contained that incarnation will be captured in engines of procreation. Technologies will become ensouled, just as souls become denatured and shifted into collective lattices rather than into the animal-hominid bodies of old evolutionary times. "Demons" will be able to take human form, and souls will be able to dwell in cognitive lattices, so it is small wonder that today's science-fiction landscape of novels and computer games is filled with mythologies of dungeons and dragons, monsters and devils. This *para*noia is crazy, but the caricatured sketch reveals an isomorphism to an evolutionary *meta*noia that is beyond anything we could call normal. One can clue into this phenomenon of cultural evolution through the paranoid caricatures of the fundamentalists—who curiously seem to object to the Luciferic New Agers more than the Ahrimanic technologists in computer science—or one can clue into it through cyberpunk fiction, or one can get more than a clue if one reads Steiner and realizes that what one is looking at in the new electronic America so celebrated and hyped by Stewart Brand and Howard Rheingold is a collectivization that can be mythologically identified as the incarnation of the demon Ahriman.

When life evolved, molecules were enclosed within the membrane of the cell; when
mind evolved, cells were enclosed within the
membrane of an individual organism. Now
a planetary entity is evolving, and individual
minds are being enclosed within a planetary
lattice. New Age folk see it as a bodhisattvaic
ideal of empathy for all sentient beings, from
whales and dolphins in the sea to starving
nomads in the Sahel; Skinheads feel it as the
power of the collective as they stomp in a
rock concert or murder and rampage around
soccer matches; scientific folk feel it as they
race to replace minds with planetary lattices
of fifth-generation computers or package nature in Biosphere II in preparation for its ex-
port to Mars.

2.

The spatialization of time in Disney World
and the confrontation with evil in the dark of
the frightful ride are forms of kitsch so artistically subtle that they have tricked intellectuals into thinking that Disneyism is beneath
their notice and definitely not worth their
time; but while they were paying attention
to more important matters of higher education, the Los Angelization of the planet was
taking place with Disneylands implanted in
Florida, Japan, and France. A new electronic
society was emerging in which the shift from
education to entertainment would surround
them with a postliterary culture in which they

would be alien immigrants from an old world. Paradoxically, while the hyperspecialized literary academics retreated into the trivia of deconstructionist and semiotic cults, Disney's Imagineers began to take on the whole world, politically and religiously. In fact, Disneyism is the world's cleverest and most successful new religion: clever, because the hundreds of millions whose lives have been touched by their time in Disney's world never became aware that they were participating in a religious celebration of life; and successful, because with its shift from socialization by fear to enculturation by fun, and its shift from life as sacrifice and renunciation to life as enjoyment and entertainment, Disneyism has converted hundreds of millions without the auric presence of a guru, the evangelical pressure of Christian indoctrination, or the shadow of an Islamic sword.

Even in the New World, the Catholic Church of my youth in the fifties in Los Angeles could not break away from the medieval social structures of princes of the Church and an infallible king upon a throne. Belonging to a time before California had hit the beach of history, it could not abandon its dark medieval fortresses of suffering, torture, and martyrdom. It knew only how to feel its military power over your life by instilling terror and demanding obedience. Through the four last things of death, judgment, heaven, and hell, it took control of your lifetime by holding the high ground of the future.

The logo for this, the world's first multi-national corporation, was not a happy mouse, but an instrument of execution. Martyrs were its heroes and sources of inspiration for countless paintings that often went into gruesome detail of the frying or dismemberment of God's most favored ones. Churches were intimidating spaces of much darkness and little light, great echoing vaults in which the leftovers of martyrdom were saved as relics to impress the unthinking and cure the faithful. By governing the body through the power of an overwhelming and impossible denial of its physical existence, the Church took control of life at its deepest roots of sex and death. But it would be the future that it presumed to control that would undo it, and while its attention was focused on stopping intellectuals from reading forbidden books and preventing lovers from having sexual relations without the conjugal bond and a commitment to reproduction, a new prophet arose in our midst in L.A. who was so deceptively camouflaged that to this day most people think of him as an enormously successful businessman and not as the influential founder of a new world religion.

If there is a family tree of world religions that keeps branching out from its primordial roots, then Catholicism is a branch of the Abrahamic trunk; Protestantism is another Christian branching out from medievalism to modernism, and America's new world visions, from Washington's Freemasonry, to

47

Whitman's erotic new age of the Body Electric, and on to Mormonism in the nineteenth century and Disneyism in the twentieth: all of these are descendants of the Rosicrucian Enlightenment,[7] and all are fruitful branches of the Reformation's idea of the worth of the individual in the new era of the Protestant Ethic and the Spirit of Capitalism. With its business visions of prosperity as evidence of divine election, the new middle class put forth a new bourgeois realism to take the place of the old medieval stained-glass visions of suffering and salvation. In Mormon temples, the murals express an earthly conception of heaven, a materialistic view of paradise that, paradoxically, is much closer to the industrial materialism of Soviet Socialist Realist painting than to the windows of a Gothic cathedral. Disneyism is a twentieth-century continuation of this American streak of populism, a civic religion similar to Mormonism in its use of a publicly accessible comic-book art to inspire the average, patriotic American citizen. Disney's vision is a solid middle-class and midwestern celebration of small-town values lifted up and preserved in the midst of that new world of the New World, the postwar Los Angeles of freeways, Hollywood, and television.

The 1950s in Los Angeles, like the 1450s in Florence, was an extraordinarily transformative time and space. L.A. was the first place to effect the shift from industrial to informational, from coal and steel to gas and

plastic, from railroads and farms to freeways
and aerospace industries, from New York's
exalted millionaires and depressed tenement
classes to suburbia's new and universal middle class. World War II had enabled the
United States to pull out of the Depression
by a clever maneuver in which it shifted its
source of economic value from the past to the
future. Traditional societies derive their value
from the legacies and inheritances of the past,
from the Magna Carta or the Constitution,
as well as from the family trust. The motto
of a traditional society is: Do not spend capital. The world is seen to be a fixed and limited system, and one is counseled to avoid
foolish risk-taking and live prudently off the
interest of the accumulated capital, intellectual and financial, of the past.

But the Depression quite literally released
the volume, heat, and pressure within the
economic engine of the traditionally ruling,
plutocratic class. By hindsight now one can
see that the Depression is not so much a single, crisp event, but rather a change in the
dynamics of the phase-space of the world
economy: an accumulation of noise in the
global economy as the dynamical system began to be pulled away from a periodic attractor, with its alternating cycles of boom
and bust, to a chaotic attractor. A chaotic
attractor is not a container filled with discrete
objects, be they gold ingots or squares of
land; it is a complex process whose phase-
space requires more than three dimensions to

generate a phase-portrait of its behavior. In
the years leading up to the Depression, the
phase-space of the world economy expanded
quickly, but it became so stretched out of its
conventionally perceived shape by the managers of capital, that people no longer could
understand the "world" they had entered.
The world could no longer be understood to
be a container, a large bank or a ruling class
that could hold the fixed values of the past.
When value could not be fixed to land or
metals, it became, not a solid like gold, or a
liquid currency like pounds and dollars, but
an expanding, highly volatile, and indeed
explosive gas. From the shock of that expansion, early capitalism experienced the
shattering of its world interpretation. The
thermodynamic heat, which had hitherto
been imagined to be contained within the elitist chamber of the ruling class, expanded into
the new phase-space of the world economy,
and the expansion of space was matched by
an acceleration of time in a shortening of the
communications interval of transaction in
that purely mental space known as "the
global market."

All kinds of new ideologies, fascist and
communist, rose up to interpret what was
basically not so much an ideological phenomenon as a topological one, one that required
not systems of linear control by party elites,
but a new mathematical imagination of the
world. The ideologists, however, were reactionary minds locked into rigid geometries

of center and periphery, of leader and masses, precisely at a time when these pie-shaped pieces of euclidean geometry could no longer map onto the phase-portraits of a world evidencing "self-organization from noise." Again, by virtue of 20/20 hindsight, one can look back to see that neither Roosevelt, Lenin, nor Hitler, really knew what was happening to him; the most accurate expression of the new systems dynamics was not coming from political and economic elites, but out of the demimonde of avant-garde musicians and black jazz. Jazz was an expression of improvisation, spontaneity, and imaginative response to given situations that cannot be controlled but can be allowed to organize themselves through expanding spaces that redefine the relation between dissonance and consonance, melodic line and harmonic state-space, noise and information. Jazz was also essentially the expression of the underdog going through a cultural transformation in which the "hot" agricultural slave became the "cool" urban artist.

51

Art, as a value, is an intellectual property; in producing wealth, the artist is a magician who makes something out of nothing, music out of noise. Whereas in early capitalism, wealth was seen to be generated by the owners of property, land and factories, in late capitalism, wealth is information that achieves value in the process of sharing it. A song unsung or a novel unread, like Berkeley's unheard tree falling in the middle of the forest,

is not art. Art becomes art in the process of
cultural exchange between artist and audi-
ence. Its value is dependent upon sharing, so
what the Depression signaled was an expansion of phase-space from the nation-state
to the world economy and a shift in our
mathematical imagination of the world. We
moved unconsciously from center-periphery
hierarchical systems of control and organization to new systems of chaos dynamics that
required a much more radical sense of participation; but consciously intellectuals re-
acted by trying to deny complexity in fascist
and communist systems in which the state
was more important than the individual or
private property. In the usual manner in
which "We become what we hate," and enemies exchange characteristics through conflict, the Second World War changed the
nature of capitalism. The communists and
fascists defined "property" in the terms of
early capitalism, but the Americans shifted to
late capitalism by extending the concept by
having the state invest in the "intellectual
property" of science. Out of this crossing of
government and science through people like
Vannevar Bush and the Office of Scientific
Information, a new systems-dynamics way
of knowing the world was created by information theory and cybernetics as articulated
by Shanon, Wiener, Von Neuman, and
McCulloch. Science began to try to catch up
with music.

Both fascism and communism are hysterical systems of control, ones that cannot tolerate humor, ambiguity, complexity, and multidimensional topologies: namely, all those qualities that are so richly present in jazz. As these hysterical ideologies sought to take control of the world through various forms of linear control in the thirties, the new world-space expressed itself in the unenlightened and tragic form of a world war. If you are not enlightened enough to understand your contradictions and out of that initiatic understanding artistically create your own destiny, then you will experience your contradictions tragically in the form of an inflicted fate. But even in its tragic form, the world war still required new world structures in which to pursue consciously national goals. Once these structures of planetization were in place, then peacetime could provide the more enlightened and expansive opportunity to extend participation in "intellectual property" in the birth of the new universal middle class that the rulers of early capitalism, as well as their reactionary opponents in fascism and communism, had aborted.

With not as much of a mental tradition rooting it to past interpretations of the world, the United States, the birthplace of jazz, shifted more easily from the past to the future as the source of its economic and spiritual value. It went into debt, created deficit spending to extend credit to the factory owners during the war, and then to the factory workers turned consumers after the war. In a tra-

ditional society, you are advised not to live
beyond your means, not to squander the resources that belong to your children and
grandchildren, but in a futuristic society, bor-
rowing is simply a way of adding on to the
family house in order to have space for the
unborn generation. By the enlightened move
of investing its identity in its former enemies,
Germany and Japan, and by domestically extending credit to its working classes, through
the patriotically disguised socialism of the
G.I. Bill for education and housing, the
United States created postindustrial society:
a society of consumption, not savings, an
expanding, polluting, noisy society of tract-
house subdivisions, shopping malls, freeways, junior colleges, state colleges, and
universities for everyone. If traditional, pre-
Depression, paper capitalism had clubby Yale
or Harvard, this new electronic society had
the new public intellectual property of Berkeley and U.C.L.A.

54

In agricultural society, the peasant is bound
by his feet to the soil; in postindustrial society
the citizen is mortgaged up to his eyeballs in
debt. Indebtedness becomes the means by
which one is embedded in the very matrix of
the expanding consumer society. The home
is no longer a multigenerational abode, the
fixed ground of value and familial identity; it
is real estate, and the family can sell and
move, changing houses the way one might
change cars or clothes. In trading up from the
old neighborhood to a better neighborhood,

the home becomes a vehicle of movement through time and space. For such a dynamically moving and informationally rich society, value is created in the process of transactions; it is not fixed to the family farm or the family trust. Those who understood this new postwar process of the creation of wealth became immensely rich, and one of the greatest geniuses of this new economy in which you become rich by investing other people's money in your own artistic ideas was Walt Disney.

The great French economic historian Fernand Braudel has noted that the Depression, which we tend to think of in terms of Wall Street stockbrokers jumping out of skyscraper windows, was actually the signal of the shift of the capital of the world economy from London to New York.[8] The Depression was also the formative event in the emergence of the civic religion of Disneyism. In the midst of the Depression, Walt Disney received his inspiration to recover the archaic through modern media; his mind drifted off into a reverie, sank to archaic levels of consciousness in totemism and animism, and resurfaced with an animated mouse. It was an inspired intuition, for the mouse is the most vulnerable of animals, and yet the most widespread, one whose habitat extends from "nature" in the country to "culture" in the city. At a time when the laboring class was shifting from country to city, this tiny symbol of physical vulnerability and unrecognized worth was bound to appeal to the masses as an archetypal symbol of their own enduring life as survivors. Mickey Mouse became the psyche of America in vaudeville blackface and white gloves.

Disney's daydream was timely, for the factories were closing, the family farm was failing, and millions of people were shifting from the rural South to the cities of the North. People were disoriented and profoundly unhappy, so Disney's religious impulse to make happiness the basic experience of human community arose precisely at a time when people were open to other modes of experience than the traditional emphases on suffering and martyrdom. The mystery school in which people could pass from misery to happiness in the Depression was, of course, the movie theater; it became the very beginning of America's rite of passage from an industrial to informational society, for the rise of the movie industry of Hollywood was to prefigure what would be repeated with television, and then again with Silicon Valley.

Even to this day, this economic prefiguring of Disneyism has not stopped, for Disney World is the greatest tourist attraction in America, and America itself is now becoming the greatest tourist attraction for affluent Europe and Asia. The largest industry in America is becoming tourism, which is another variant of the entertainment industry, the Hollywood that gives birth to Disneyland. America has sloughed off its old industries of material production to Japan and Korea, and through the global broadcasting of its American system of information, culture, and values, it is recapitulating its earlier shift from industrial to informational. The materialist seeks to gain economic value from the mining of limited resources; the autopoietic (self-making) capitalist creates value through artistic transformation, through the alchemical transformation of lead into gold, sound into music. The factories in the United States of the twenty-first century are more likely to be technical and artistic studios than the steel mills and assembly plants of Japan and Korea. With electronic miniaturization bringing technicians and designers together in small and highly skilled, artistic teams, mass production of widgets will not be an attractive economic enterprise for advanced countries such as the U.S.A.

Before the War in the Gulf, industrial economists, such as Sony's Chairman Akio Morita or Mitterrand's adviser Jacques Attali, saw the nineties as the period of the economic decline of America and the emergence of a new global magnetic field polarized between Western Europe and Japan.[9] But neither France, Germany, nor Japan was able to respond to the world's first post–Cold War crisis in Kuwait, and as Germany and Japan stood by, motionless, France did not know which way to turn. Its Gaullist foreign policy had been founded on positioning itself to become the scientific center for the Arab world, and its Defense Minister was openly pro Iraq. Mitterrand had to decide whether to continue to listen to Attali about the United States' decline, or change course and jettison the old Gaullist foreign policy. Faced with a choice between being pro Iraq or pro United States, Mitterrand abandoned his Defense Minister and ran to catch up with the partnership of Bush and Major, for the economic facts of life are that the new Disneyland being constructed near Paris represents the largest foreign investment in France in its entire history. The linear extrapolations of geopolitics made by Jacques Attali were like the ones made in the seventies, when pundits said that by 1990 all the dollars of the world would be in OPEC's coffers. Morita sees Japan's buying up of CBS and Rockefeller Center as symbols of America's decline; he doesn't recognize that Japan has been suckered into buying up America's old symbols from the communication systems of the thirties, but America is using the money to generate new planetary mythological systems.

In planetization, the phase-portrait of the world cannot be held within the geometry of behavior of a single center in New York. The economy of the world is a polycentric topology, and its accurate phase-portrait would require drawing in many centers. The demand for entrance into the world game signaled by social revolutions in Eastern Europe and indebtedness in Latin America are signs of expansion of the phase-space of the world economy. For America to try to hold on to the national system of world hegemony expressed by either the Radio City 1930s or the Sixth Avenue 1960s row of corporate headquarters would be stupid and futile; but, obviously, the Rockefellers understand this in the very act of selling half of Rockefeller Center to the Japanese for a very high price precisely at the instant before Manhattan real estate values went into a sharp decline. Jacques Attali talked of centers and peripheries, and his mathematical imagination was still Cartesian and all too Parisian, and although he fondly predicted the decline of America, he had little understanding of the posthistoric phenomenon that is America.

The "buying up" of "American" resources by "foreign" corporations is simply yet another expression of planetization. The true historic interface now is not between the American and the foreign corporation, but between the world economy and the biosphere in our coming to a new understanding of planetary dynamics in which pollution becomes the new source of improvisation, the new "ground" for economic value. Periods of a frontier expansion into new space are, of necessity, followed by periods of consolidation into institutional forms. This cultural shift involves a movement from an expanding economy that pollutes by mining resources, to a consolidating economy that mines pollution to produce new intellectual properties, such as John Todd's "Living Machines" in which plants, bacteria, and sunlight are orchestrated into biological consorts that digest pollution.[10]

The postindustrial Los Angeles of subdivisions and freeways and a universal middle class has now become a Third World city of eighty languages, visible decay of social systems, youth gang warfare fought with machine guns, and environmental collapse in the lack of water and clean air. In the fifties, no one worried about living in a desert with a way of life that called for sweeping the sidewalk with a garden hose, washing the car every week, and having swimming pools in middle-class backyards and fountains in air-conditioned shopping malls. Now Los Angeles, just like São Paolo or Mexico City, is having to think about the underdogs, of immigrants and environments.

This expansion of the field of perception will require a transformation of mentality, a new sensitivity to noise and pollution as undeveloped resources: not a "return to nature" in a preindustrial mentality, but a transformation of our consciousness of just what exactly constitutes "nature." In industrial society, fortunes were created from the transport systems for conscious bodies in the railways; in postindustrial society, fortunes were created from the transport systems of cars and jets; but in metaindustrial culture the fortunes will be made from the transport systems for unconscious bodies, for the waste and pollution we pushed into the shadows.

Frankly, although I have lived in Europe and have traveled to Japan, in this reconstitution of "nature" in which pollution becomes for a metaindustrial society what the soil was for an agricultural society, I do not see either Morita's Japan or Attali's France as being more advanced than the United States.

The United States and here I mean the culture, and decidedly not the politicians, is just too wild and noisily creative for anyone to be able to predict its future. Groups within the U.S.A. are thinking about "nature" in a radical, posthistoric way, and only the U.S.A. is crazy and risk-taking enough to shift so much of its resources away from nationally managed and industrially produced goods to informationally generated planetary mythological systems. This move is so historically unprecedented that it is impossible to predict, as Attali thought he could, just how it is going to turn out.

Certainly, if the nineteenth-century world of Grimm's folk tales, that archaic landscape of beauty and cruelty, could end up as the twentieth-century polity of German fascism, then so could the 1950s world of Disney end up in the nineties in a new and more marketable version of electropop fascism: a gigantic Plato's Cave amusement-park ride in which Barbie Dolls' Ken becomes handsome President Quayle for an American polity in which Fun and Entertainment, not torture and suffering, are used to contain people and hold them in the suspended animation of

61

happiness. Or we could end up in some visionary New Age with a Green government in a sci-fi and intradimensional, dolphin-torn, whale-sounded, galactic musical polity of extraterrestrial consciousness.

Unfortunately, in our dark comedy of errors in the Sunbelt there is more evidence for pessimism than for my optimistic hope that the dark age of vidiocy is transitory. It does indeed look as if the United States is irreversibly committed to the electropop fascism of patriotic Fun and Entertainment as the only way of holding a continental and polycultural nation together. Although the Greens may talk about the cultural diversity of having a "Europe of the Regions," and envision a transformed North America of autonomous regions such as the Hopi Nation and Quebec, the War in the Gulf has energized the cultural simplifications of a yellow-ribboned patriotism. Learning new languages and studying other cultures takes time, hard work, and an attention span that is now physiologically impossible for children raised on *Sesame Street*, commercials, and MTV.

For people of my generation, radio stimulated a deeply interior and private space that we filled with the creations of our own imaginations, but MTV is a visual crowd that does not allow solitude or imagination. Listen to the songs of Suzanne Vega—"Tom's Diner," for example—and then watch the music-video version. You will see every poetic image and sensitive nuance of rhythm destroyed

by one fashion-magazine snapshot after another. What the media engineers do to the
lyrics of the song, they also do to the words
and philosophy of the Constitution. But with
a handsome and likeable President like
Quayle, we could look good even in our decline. As education declines, patriotic Americans can suck down a few beers and toast the
flag with a hearty commercial: "This Bud's
for you, America!"

To reverse this cultural slide, we would
have to learn from the first Depression and
the world war that followed it. Instead of
trying to retreat in fear into hysterical fun-
damentalisms, be they Christian, Islamic, or
Marxist, we have to expand our imaginations
in synchrony with the expansion of the phase-
space of our new global economy, technology, and culture. Just as once before in the
forties we extended credit to an underclass
and invested our identity in our enemies, so
now will we have to do that once again in
the nineties. Now the underclass is not simply
the American working class, but the bottom
of the hemispheric south and the fundamental
ground of the global ecology. If, once again,
America invests its identity in its former enemy, as Secretary of State James Baker seems
to have done with the Soviet Union, then we
might be able to experience the period of the
consolidation into form in two pulses.

The first pulse in the early nineties, after
the reunification of Germany, was the cultural consolidation of European civilization,

a civilization that went all around the world, eastward from Vancouver to Vladivostock. Unfortunately, this post–Cold War reunification of European civilization summoned forth the ancient shadow of Europe in the form of Islam. Saddam Hussein's dream of an Arab Nation was a real threat to Europe, and that was why those parts of the Arab world around the Mediterranean that wanted to be part of the superpower of Europe 1992—Egypt, Morocco, Turkey, and Syria —lined up against Iraq and its vision of a renascent Islam that could fill the void left by a supposedly declining American world hegemony.

Before we can have a truly new world system to replace the old Cold War polarization, we have to deal with this old karma of the Crusades and the wars of modernism against medievalism. As a medieval mentality of rigid geometries, Islamic fundamentalism is attractive to people who cannot understand our contemporary transition from the linear mathematical mentality of Galileo's dynamics and Newton's calculus to chaos dynamics and the new sciences of complexity. Fundamentalism, of any variety, is the rigid shadow of this new flexible mentality of the electronic arts and the mathematics of chaos.

The last world transition required a global depression and a world war; the purpose of the New Age movement of the seventies, as articulated by modest and sensible people such as Esalen's Michael Murphy or Findhorn's David Spangler, was to enable us to become enlightened enough to effect the transition without the literalism of another depression and world war. Unfortunately, fundamentalists are precisely those sorts of folks who prefer to take things literally and, therefore, insist on having just those sorts of externally tragic events, such as world wars, as the only way in which they can let go of the old and evolve into the new.

If the United Nations, and not merely the United States sucking down some Buds and kicking some butt, can integrate the underdog Palestinians and Arabs into the new world civilization, then we will be able to take an enlightened step away from the cultural entropy of global religious warfare from Ireland to Indonesia to Idaho. If we take the high road and don't relive the Crusades or the Thirty Years' War all over again, then the second pulse of global transformation, around the turn of the millennium, would be "the Gaia Politique,"[11] the reconstitution of the world economy in the biosphere in a rearticulation of the cultural relationships between the northern and southern hemispheres. Just as before, when we refused to extend participation in the expanding phase-space of the world economy, we experienced our contradictions as an economic depression and a world war, now, as we are refusing to extend participation in the expanding phase-space of the global electronic economy, we are experiencing our contradictions in the form of planetary ecological damage and Third World participation in the global flow of currencies through the shadow economy of the drug traffic. The drug traffic is a shadow economy that outlines a real emergent form, the collapse of the postwar doctrine of development; it is noise that has to be transformed into information. We recognize that the Cold War is over, but we have not yet recognized that its related 1940s concept of Third World development is also over.

In the ending of the Cold War there are some healthy signs that the United States has come to a new understanding of both the artistic nature of an autopoietic economy, and the psychological nature of the Enemy. All during the War in the Gulf, we kept affirming that the Iraqi people were not an enemy. This is a giant cultural step forward from the days of my youth when the movies taught us how to hate the Japs, Germans, and Korean gooks. During the Cold War, in order to be able to make the transition from a past-oriented economy of fixed values, to an autopoietic economy of values created in transaction through indebtedness to the future, the United States needed an intimate partner to create that medium of exchange, and that intimate partner was the Enemy. The great era of American world hegemony, of cars open to the sun, was also the dark era of Cold War terror and the battle against the hated Enemy —the Commies. In a social construction of

culture as pure mythology, the interpretation
of the world was then a paranoid narrative of
the Communist World Conspiracy. As a pa-
rochial school child at meetings of my Catholic Sodality, I was given right-wing comic
books that showed the Russians paratrooping
into the backyard, and commissars hanging
priests from the lampposts. At the edge of
my child's world there was this vast, two-
headed Asiatic monster of Russia and China,
and this nightmarish beast was under the dic-
tatorial control of Satanic people like Stalin
with his armies and H-bombs and Beria with
his secret police. Not just my child's world,
but our entire postwar world economy was
supported by this fear of the Enemy. The
U.S.A. could have lost a few states, such as
North Dakota or Alabama, and never missed
them, but if we had lost the Russians as our
enemy, our whole economy with its new
California aerospace industries would have
collapsed. Without this fear of the Enemy,
the average citizen, with his anti-intellectual
fear of literary eggheads and Dr. Frankenstein
scientists, would never have voted for the
massive deficit spending that was needed to
support Cold War science. Now we are
slightly more enlightened, and Gorbachev is
basically saying: "Look, since we Russians
have been supporting your economy all
along, it is about time you shared the wealth
in a less unconscious form. Let's have a
joint American-Soviet expedition to Mars."
Quayle doesn't understand the historical op-

67

portunity of the offer, and he wants to plant the American flag on Mars,[12] for his mind (if I may be forgiven the hyperbole) is still locked into the Cold War of the fifties; he would like to see a return of the Enemy and the good old days of American world hegemony, and so he hopes that the Russian right wing will knock off or absorb Gorbachev so that the Cold War can come back without the Republicans getting blamed for it. But Gorbachev's proposal for a joint U.S.-U.S.S.R space program is a good one, for a truly planetary culture does require a postnational movement into a new space, as well as an enlightenment in which one's enemy is recognized to be an intimate part of the architecture of one's own consciousness. Ironically, old right-wing, capitalist Disney was a preparation for this new post–Cold War world, and Southern California's Ronald Reagan was just the President to effect this unconscious transformation. In the cultural shift from theory to practice, actor Reagan is to artist Disney what Lenin was to Marx.

3.

Although literary intellectuals of my ilk may write books expressing snobbish disgust with this new polity, no book will ever put this electronic cultural transformation into reverse. We will have this polity of mediocracy in which imagineers manipulate images for the electropeasantry as long as we have television as our dominant form of communication. It will do no good to try to create some new Amish Lancaster County in which there is no TV, for that quaint space will only become yet another movie set of heritage and tradition in the midst of the vast electronic polity. It will only be when television is superceded by some new technology of communication, just as television superceded print, that we will have a new noetic polity created by the new means of communication. When that happens, humanity will probably look back upon the age of television as a dark age. And if we stop to consider both Marshall McLuhan's and Jean Gebser's theories of the evolution of communication and consciousness, then we can see that a dark age is always the signal of the change of state from one level of consciousness to another.

The shift from what Jean Gebser called the Archaic structure to the Magical was marked by the dark age of the emergence of warfare, and archaeologists find places like Hacilar to be littered with corpses, attesting to the effectiveness of the sling and the bow and arrow used, not as weapons of the Mesolithic hunt for animals, but as Neolithic weapons of war.[13] In the shift from Gebser's Magical to Mythical structure of consciousness, which is chronicled in the literature of Hesiod and Homer, we have the Aegean dark age from roughly 1000 B.C.E. to the Athenian florescence of Aeschylus and Plato in the fifth century B.C.E. In the shift from the Mythical to

the Mental structure of consciousness, we
have the Dark Ages of Europe. And in our
shift from Gebser's Mental to Integral structure of consciousness, we have the electronic
dark age of America, in which the media dis-
solve the Mental structures of modernist, European thought, but cannot create the Integral
level of evolutionary consciousness as prophesied by Gebser or Sri Aurobindo.[14]

In the dark age at the end of the Archaic
structure, magical signs and iconic notation
appeared, and this paved the way for writing.
At the end of the Magical structure, first syl-
labic and then alphabetic writing appeared,
and this paved the way for hieratic, mytho-
poeic thought. At the end of the Mythical
structure, print appeared, and this paved the
way for the decline of priestcraft and the rise
of modern art and science. Now at the end
of print, electronics appears and seems to be
paving the way for the musical polities of the
future. I envision these musical polities as
vibratory pulses of light and sound that generate fields of incarnation not bound to territorial modes of identity, be these the turf of
nation-states or the flesh of individuals. In this
evolutionary emergence it is not the literary
intelligentsia of *The New York Review of Books*
that is bringing forth this new culture, for it
is as repugnant to them as the Reformation
was to the Catholic Church. These spooky
transpersonal, transnational, cyberspace networks of artificial intelligence and fiber-optic
planetary lattices of light often can be

glimpsed at the edges of our cultural imagination by considering what we literary intellectuals find to be humanly repellent, ugly,
or evil.

Gebser and Aurobindo only envision the
angelic, "Supramental" pole of this emergent
field of the Integral level of consciousness,
but there is a demonic, cyberpunk pole as
well. To focus only on "the Descent of the
Supramental" in the New Age is as one-sided
as seeing that other New Age of the seven-
teenth century only as A. N. Whitehead's
"Century of Genius" and not also as the
brutal and savage Thirty Years' War in which
Rosicrucian Heidelberg and Prague are destroyed by the Catholic armies of the Counter-
Reformation. Descartes was a genius, but he
was also a soldier stationed in Prague.[15] This
new cyberpunk, technological culture is
brought forth by Top and Pop, electronic
science and pop music, and both the hackers
and the rockers are anti-intellectual and un-
sympathetic to the previous Mental level
expressed by the genius of European
civilization.

It is easy for literary intellectuals living in
New York or Europe to write sarcastic essays
on Disney World, but the truth is that the
dumb know something that the smart do not:
namely that the intellect is not an adequate
instrument with which to sound the depths
of the universe. With more than 100,000
books published each year, no leader or citizen can be responsibly informed, and no lit-

erate intellectual can pretend that he is well read and learned, even were he or she to read 24 hours a day. When a system goes into overload, the noise begins to build up, and it is noise that draws a system from one attractor to another. To be a European intellectual now is to be like a Pharisee at the time of Jesus, or a Catholic Inquisitor at the time of Galileo. Professor Richard Rorty goes to great lengths to prove that philosophy is all washed up, and then when he realizes that he has just talked himself out of his job as a tenured professor of philosophy, he quickly backs up and says that, nevertheless, one must continue "the Discourse of the West." This is not the voice of an explorer of the dimensions of consciousness in the universe; it is the frustrated shriek of a pettifogging clerk who has spilled his files of the received opinions of his superiors. It is precisely "discourse" that is being transformed by the present culture, and as for that fiction of the past called "the West," that classical stage set of the old European ruling class always had to be seen from one angle only to maintain the illusion of depth. Anyone who ever bothered to look outside the bound covers of the mind of a Benjamin Jowett or an F. M. Cornford discovered the cultural history of the Semitic Phoenicians and the black Africans in the formation of Egyptian and Aegean civilizations.[16]

What is unique to the European cultural experiment called America is an anti-European, anti-intellectual, anti-Mental, and anti-natural level of cultural evolution. For aging literary intellectuals such as I, ones born into a time when writers such as William Faulkner and T. S. Eliot were living giants of immense cultural authority, figures whose transcontinental shadows could block out and obscure the unique nature of the time in which I was coming of age in the Los Angeles of 1954— for our kind, it is too late, and we cannot participate in this new electronic mediocracy any more than the monks at Lindisfarne in 793 could participate in the Viking Terror that sacked their monastery and announced the beginning of the maritime projection of Europe into what was to become the civilization spread around the shores of the Atlantic.

The transition from the Mental culture of Europe to this new Integral culture of the twenty-second century is clearly a literary dark age, and what these dark shadows black out are writers. Editors in New York now use the phrase "literary essay" as a term of derision, for no American publisher wants a V. S. Pritchett in the age of John Naisbitt. A literary prose style actually gets in the public's way, for it causes journalists to trip up on the play of words and the presence of complexity when they are simply trying to figure out what slogan to use to catch what the book is trying to sell. The most marketable prose now is a dehydrated general nonfiction slurry that has to include shelf-life additives put in by editors and packaging by the sales department so that it can be quickly microwaved in two-minute radiations on TV talk shows. Of course, these microwaved celebrities grow cold just as fast as they grew hot, but that doesn't matter, for though celebrities come and go, the factories, studios, and publicity houses that produce them remain and continue to sustain Manhattan lifestyles for the celebrity distributors. Philosophy, literature, and art cannot survive in this world of promotional tours, shopping malls, and bookstores in supermarkets, and so it only remains for my generation to pass on so that no one will remember a time before *Sesame Street* and MTV.

Small wonder, then, that literary intellectuals become reactionaries, for it is so comforting to be a reactionary, as it allows one to feel morally superior as one bears one's "chalice through a throng of foes." But the more one closes up into this defensive posture of the moralist, the more the mystical revelations of the future have to force us open by appearing in their demonic guise as the ugly and the evil; and yet the ugly and the evil are really only reflections of us, of our moralistic refusal to evolve. Recall that the monsters in science fiction films are often lizards, and you will recognize a mammal's way of looking back on evolution and rewriting natural history.

74

My friend Wendell Berry has become perhaps the most outspoken critic of this new
electronic society; he has pronounced anathema on our contemporary techno-world of
low kitsch and high tech, and has made much
of his refusal to own a TV or write with a
computer.[17] Wendell is a farmer in Kentucky;
he works like a farmer, but he also thinks like
a farm: too many fences that keep out both
the Wild and the high cultures of Europe and
Asia. Wendell has created a beautiful way of
life for himself behind those fences, with
good books to furrow his brow and fine Bel-
gian draft horses to plow his furrows, but on
the walls that keep the modern world at a
proper distance, you'll find an English country squire's collection of the works of other
poets and moralists, such as Milton and Pope,
but not much of modern science, Continental
philosophy, or Eastern mysticism. It's a no-
bler way of life than most of us have been
blessed to create, but there's not much of a
future for this way of living behind fences.

The traditional family farm is a place where
God is a man who knows how to keep
women and animals in their place. If they
know what is best for them, then the man
tells them that animals and women are really
more fulfilled in this sacramental life that con-
sumes them in, and as, the preparation of
food. That was my father's world on his parent's farm in Indiana, a world he left behind
to go to Theodore Dreiser's Chicago, and
that Chicago was another world that I left

behind when my parents moved me to Walt
Disney's Los Angeles. For most of my life,
I have recoiled in revulsion from Los Angeles
and tried to get back to some comfortable
world that could be called a home, first in
my ancestral Ireland and now in the even
more ancient Celtic heartland of Switzerland.
But settling down never lasts, for time is
change, and there is no such steady-state
thing as "nature." The idea of "the balance of
nature" is another one of those cultural fic-
tions like Rorty's "Discourse of the West."[18]
Nature is the horizon of culture; as we move,
it moves too and becomes a new nature that
some would call unnatural. Nature includes
the molecules electrically dancing in the toxic
dump and the supernova polluting a galaxy
with radiation. What Bill McKibben tends to
think of as nature in his Adirondack musings
for *The New Yorker* and his book *The End of
Nature*,[19] owes far more to the culture of
Sierra Club calendars, the photographs of
Ansel Adams, and the paintings of Constable
and Caspar David Friedrich than it does to
the cosmic activities of the Creator. Similarly, Wendell Berry's image of nature is a
cultural construction, a freeze-frame of time;
its image is beautifully captured on the cover
of his new book *What Are People For?* in the
painting by Thomas Hart Benton of "Politics, Farming, and Law in Missouri." It is
America around the time Wendell was born,
the world that vanished in the Depression; it

is the preelectronic world that was electronically re-created by Walt Disney. As artists,
Wendell and Walt are just about mirror op-
posites of one another, for the patrician poet
creates a noble character out of the past that
tries to stand up and stand in for the Creator,
but through his fidelity to the discourse of
the past he conceals the time we are living in,
a time when George Bush and Saddam Hussein fight it out on CNN. The master of kitsch
mass produces caricatures that dance for public recreation, but in their deception they reveal our invisible cultural transformation: the
reconstitution of "nature" through electronic
culture. Thus in the fixing of time in human
perception, the fake becomes the exposure of
the hidden, and the authentic becomes the
concealment of the real.

Wendell Berry is a moralist, and the moralist tends to think that the laws of God are
more on his side than on his enemy's, so he
will try through faith in religion and the exercise of ritual to get God to settle down with
him and go along with his way of life. The
mystic, however, is not a moralist, for motion, complexity, and an angelic-demonic
ambiguity in which one's enemy is also part
of the divine manifestation in history are all
part of the cosmic life on the other side of the
fence. Home means a lot to moralists, but the
mystic is society's alien and is not allowed to
have a home smaller than the universe, and
any time he tries to settle for less, to settle

down, and to set up fences, God appears as the moving whirlwind. The Book of Job, as the mystical Blake knew only too well when he decided to illustrate that text, is the mystic's reply to the moralist.

So, call me an optimist in that I blindly choose to see our dark ages as temporary, give or take a century or two. And put me down as a patriot who saw in the repellent, ugly, and evil of our American society a revelation of a planetary culture approaching us on the other side of catastrophic transformation. America's critical role in the planetization of humanity does seem to be that of the catalytic enzyme that breaks down all the traditional cultures of the world, be they Asiatic, Islamic, or European. With Disneyland in Paris and Tokyo, the United States is well on its way to dissolving all the world cultures, and I do not think that any nativistic revolt of Islam will succeed in stopping it any more than Marxist-Leninism did. The present-day nativistic attacks of Islam against the airlines are, like the Ghost Dance of the Plains Indians against the railroads, just simply not powerful enough to stop the electronic spread of Disneyism, Hollywood movies and TV programs, rock and roll, Coca-Cola, and McDonald's.

We can despair at this trashing of the world, and in our bitterness curse the age, for writers are good with words and will always find it easier to criticize and curse; but if we lift our imagination into the whirlwind

that takes our home away, we might just see
for a moment with the eye of the hurricane
to experience a planetary atmosphere at work
on the little things we ignored and the big
things we never knew.

CNN: THE AMERICAN REPLACEMENT OF HISTORICAL REALITY

When we look up at the night sky, time becomes space, as many different times are spread out before us, for the stars we are seeing do not reveal the light of the present but the past; the emanations of the celestial present that are light-years away from Earth will not reach us until the future. It is much the same with history. When we look out on contemporary events, we do not see the present, we see the past. And so the young marched in peace demonstrations against the War in the Gulf because they were seeing Vietnam, President Bush marched in with the military because he was seeing World War II, and Saddam Hussein dug in to fight in the trenches because he was seeing World War I.

When we look at TV, space becomes time, as many different places become the electronic now. Everything is going on in this same now, no matter whether the space is Baghdad, Tel Aviv, Riyadh, Dhahran, Washington, or San Diego. The diverse cultures are all in different historical time zones, tribal, preindustrial, industrial, or postindustrial, but television makes them all cutouts in an electronic collage that is *now*.

For a person born before the age of television, history is a line. For a Christian it is a line that moves from left to right on a page, from B.C. to A.D. For a person with a literary sensibility, history is a realm of the spirit, a transcendental realm of meaning that is to the present what the spoken language is to the written. The ego is fixed to the body, but the spirit is vast. The word in ink is fixed to the page, but the English language lives in the transcendental realm of the sacred past, from Churchill to Jefferson to Shakespeare and on back to *The Anglo-Saxon Chronicle*. When I sit in a living room in Zurich, watching Atlanta's CNN and listening to Senator Byrd make a speech in Washington, I am observing a gentleman of the old school, a creature from the preelectronic culture, one who had Latin as a schoolboy and so looks out at the present with a knowledge of the classics. In considering our present conflict between two cultures, European and Islamic, Senator Byrd's mind is taken back even beyond the Crusades to the battle between the Roman and Semitic peoples for control of the Mediterranean world. His address to his fellow senators refers to the Punic Wars of Romans and Carthaginians, of Hannibal and the battle of Cannae; and the cadence and syntax of his speech is so slow and thoughtful that he seems like a man from the past. And he is.

For a person with a TV sensibility, syntactical thought, that kind of periodic sentence that might come from the pages of Hooker's *The Laws of Ecclesiastical Polity*, that kind of sentence structure that is more architecture than message, that noble procession of the English language that has nave and bay and whose main idea proceeds inexorably toward the high altar, but whose stately procession does not hesitate to pause and swing the censer in the bays that hold monuments of the culture's saints and knights that made the edifice possible: such syntactical thought is not possible for a person of today. Senator Byrd could never become President because he is a foreigner in his own culture. Bush, who has difficulty completing a sentence longer than a sound-bite, is a man for our time and speaks to our TV-shortened attention span. His mind is a collage of historical fragments, and he can refer to "the vision thing," but can neither inspire nor express it.

In the television trivialization of history in which great works of art are used as signs and not symbols, the transcendental world of spirit is no longer a world of meaning, as it is for Senator Byrd and was for President Lincoln, for the symbol is merely a traffic sign of agreed upon collective meaning that organizes the movement of a people. So leaders do not symbolize or inspire, they signal. Saddam said "jihad" to signal that his people could feel good about going to war. And Bush said "going the extra mile for peace" so that his people could feel good about going to war. Since measured words and thoughts that take time to be extended into philosophies can no longer inspire or even be experienced, we need the drug of an image injected into our existential vacuum. So electronic technicians construct a music video of war, and as CNN rolled the credits, they cut to images of laser-guided bombs in black and white, then color for planes taking off from carriers, then to a commercial for *Max and Helen*, a Turner Home Entertainment made-for-television movie about the Jews and the Nazis, which we were told is "a true story." It is hard to put a frame around the frame of the TV screen, to tell what is news, what is historical reality (whatever that is), and what is entertainment.

Since war is imaginatively exciting and encourages would-be soldiers to enlist, the line is never clear between play and reality in a culture, and sports and movies teach us how to live through death. People in suburban New Jersey were shocked when a couple of thirteen-year-olds defaced a synagogue with Nazi swastikas and anti-Semitic slogans, but if the adults in Hollywood have made so much money with the Nazis, why should we be surprised when kids in the hormonic rush of puberty turn history into a Halloween costume parade for skinheads and heavy-metal freaks. Jew and Nazi, cowboy and Indian, CNN's American and Iraqi, or Disney's Pirates of the Caribbean—what's the difference? With its dramatic drumroll and lettering of **THE WAR in the GULF**, CNN's news looks just like a commercial for another made-for-television docudrama. We begin to wonder if Saddam in his bunker, watching the war on CNN, called Ted Turner on his hot line to sell the movie rights to his life. Since Turner already has so much public-domain footage in the can, it should not be hard to construct a docudrama collage for another winter's season.

The War in the Gulf will make not just one movie, but a whole genre of them, like the Western. The Muslim terrorist has become the new Indian, a straggler in an archaic culture that can be caricatured by Hollywood. Where once the Hollywood Indians whooped and hollered their savage war cries, the made-for-television Muslims will be made to shout their medieval war cries of *Allahu Akbar* as they attack the airlines as once the Indians attacked the railways. Once, a continent was crossed by rail and telegraph, now it is the planet that is encircled by satellites and uplinks and fiber-optic cables that equally displace the aboriginal nationals. The entrepreneurs of another era were great railroad barons, but now they are, in an ironically Islamic term, media moguls. Ted Turner, a curious cross between Boone Pickens the corporate raider and Jane Fonda the New Age liberal, is both billionaire and environmentalist committed to an ecological ethic and a global ethos. As a visionary capitalist, he is the true dharma heir in the esoteric lineage of Walt Disney. One began with cartoons, the other with news; both became more emblematic of the cultural shift from industrial commodities to informational properties than traditional captains of industry in steel and oil.

The railways were linear and led to the displacement of all aboriginal cultures. We ended up with a lily-white and sterile suburban culture, whereas we could have had a polyculture as rich and diverse as Europe's. Television, however, is not linear, and cable television has enabled other languages to survive in North American cities. While CNN is spreading American accents around the world, it is also spreading alien ideas within America and dissolving its small-town cultural boundaries and identities. When one listened to the Iraqi Ambassador to the United Nations and then the President of the United States, the dominance of ideology in those nation-state commercials was lessened and it was the sheer presence of the global informational technology that brought forth the new planetary noetic polity. McLuhan was right, the medium is the message. TV is unconscious architecture.

When a society is no longer constructed out of symbols, it decays into a collective constructed out of signals. "Reality" is the first casualty of this new encoding in which experience becomes information processed.

When symbol becomes reduced to sign, civilization becomes reduced to collective, and it becomes almost impossible to hold on to a philosophy, a religion, or a way of life in which one can validate that peculiar oxymoron, "a just war." A just war is just war. In an electronic culture, one cannot think, one can only entertain ideas.

When a way of life is replaced by a lifestyle, then a war between two conflicting lifestyles cannot possibly be just or unjust. There are simply two differently signaling collectives in conflict, and in the images and sound-bites they construct, they hurl the same meaningless language back and forth at one another. So old cultures are used as reference points as one side accuses the other of "savagery" or "barbarism." Bush and Saddam are not men or representatives of philosophies, they are signs carried in the streets. If a writer tries to enter into the cyberspace of the CNN electronic collage to determine right and wrong, he or she gets nowhere, so one has to fall back into one's collective to make one's way by following the signs. If you are an Arab, then the air attack on Lebanon by Israeli jets in June of 1982 is a barbarous attack on civilians. If you are an Israeli, then the 1991 Scud missile attack on Tel Aviv in which civilians are killed is a barbarous attack. Who is right, the Israelis, or the Arabs? Which war is just?

War is a peculiar kind of cultural exchange in which both sides are generally wrong but feel themselves to be morally right. Whatever valid moral difference may have existed at the start of a conflict is soon lost as the very process of conflict makes enemies resemble one another. "We become what we hate." Bush gave out the propaganda that was appropriate for an elected leader dependent upon media images and public-opinion polls, and Saddam gave out the medieval rhetoric appropriate for an Islamic military hero trying to incite the masses to jihad. Both leaders were lying, of course, but in Bush's case, since this was our collective, this was particularly sad, because the War in the Gulf was not Vietnam, and he was not LBJ. Saddam Hussein *was* a danger to world order in ways that Ho Chi Minh never was or ever could be.

Although I was a peacenik during the Vietnam War, I was astonished to find myself unable to be a dove in the Gulf War, for I feared that if the Security Council of the United Nations were unable to enforce its resolution, then we would enter a dark age of universal ethnic violence. If we are to progress from an electronic collective held together by flashing signs to a planetary culture of more individually enlightened consciousness, then we need to have another renaissance on the other side of this last crusade. In the Middle Ages, Europe was primitive and ignorant and Islam was scientifically and culturally more advanced. Out of that conflict in which Europe was the mother and Islam was the father was born the culture of Renaissance Europe, a new humanistic and scientific culture that was neither Catholic nor Muslim. Out of the War in the Gulf between an electronically denatured European civilization and a militaristically denatured religion, I was for the United Nations because I hope we will see a new planetary culture that is beyond the philosophically shallow technique of the West and the hysterically fanatic ideologies of the Near East. To effect this transformation, the United Nations had to defeat Saddam and should now create the United Nations' first planetary city-state out of Jerusalem and the entire West Bank. If Saddam had won, then millions of Islamic children would have grown up convinced that the military hero was the model, and we would have had generations of warfare everywhere and a global dark age, darker than the one that came after the disintegration of the Roman Empire.

And so I was astonished to find myself, formerly a dove in the sixties, almost a hawk in the nineties; but, of course, "dove" and "hawk" are signs and not symbolic systems that can determine the difference between right and wrong. I would rather be an owl than either a hawk or a dove. In the Gulf War, as in most, being patriotic was not being right; it was simply signaling membership in one's collective. I would have liked to be patriotic and respect my President, but it was

difficult when he behaved more like the Director of the CIA than President of the Republic.

Although Bush likes to camouflage his politics with populist metaphors taken from
sports, he is actually a member of the privileged ruling class and instinctively will only
discuss geopolitics with candor concerning
the real issues with other members of the
Club. The rest of us are treated to propaganda
and sound-bites. So Bush talked about peace
in public and war in private. With the two
armies in place and poised for war in January,
it might have seemed better to the rest of us
for Bush to hold off from war and hold out
a U.N. Peace Conference before rather than
after the conflict, as Saddam Hussein re-
quested. But for members of the Club such
a conference would have promoted Saddam
into the position of world leader and equal to
the President of the United States, and it
would have left Saddam and his military
forces intact and closer to the nuclear and
poison gas capability that could alter the geopolitics, not simply of the region, but of the
world. When the news came out of Saddam's
efforts to build a huge cannon capable of
bombarding Israel with poison gas artillery
shells, Bush, most probably, decided to go
to war to take Saddam out of the game.

We will have to wait for historians to determine whether Bush and Baker set Saddam
up by telling the American Ambassador to
Iraq, April Glaspie, to inform Saddam that

the United States was not interested in inter-
Arab squabbles, such as his argument with
Kuwait over oil-price fixing. It would seem
from the distance of my perspective, far removed from the academic think tanks and
boardrooms of power, that Saddam was
something of a country bumpkin who did not
understand the kind of hardball game that
Texas oilmen such as Bush and Baker knew
how to play, and that he fell into one trap
after another: first, by obligingly invading
Kuwait, then by helping Bush organize his
European allies by taking European families
as hostages and parading them on TV, and
then by digging in to fight World War III
with World War I's concepts and strategies.

Perhaps if Dukakis had been elected, Saddam's tactics might have enabled him to hold
Kuwait and take Mecca; but he couldn't have
picked a less likely opponent for his strategy
or a worse time to make his major move, for
Bush was precisely the kind of CIA Director
who could seek to lure Saddam into a trap
before he had time to finish his development
of nuclear weapons. But even with "naked
aggression" exposed to the world, Bush still
needed time to get the coalition together and
the military ready, and so diplomacy, as long
as it failed, served his purpose. For public
consumption, Bush gave out sound-bites
about "going the extra mile for peace," but
made certain that the chances for international
diplomacy were reduced to a hockey face-off
in Geneva between the Arab shame-culture

of Aziz and the Texas machismo of Baker. Bush's advisers knew very well that when you force an Arab leader into a corner and give him a choice of global humiliation or apotheosis through martyrdom on the battlefield, the Arab will always choose apotheosis through death in "the Mother of Battles." President Bush's letter of ultimatum with its demand for a retreat to the *status quo ante* was clearly meant to push the Iraqis into a war. If Saddam had surprised everyone by bowing to American demands and withdrawing from Kuwait, then the Arab masses would have lost a hero and the old ruling world order would have been affirmed, as the threat to American hegemony was put off. Saddam did not retreat, and so he was made to appear as the intransigent one, and his belligerence provided another occasion for Bush to invoke images of Hitler's invasion of Czechoslovakia.

With Germany reunited and making its own deal with the Soviet Union, it was moving into position to become the architect of the reconstruction of Eastern Europe, an Eastern Europe that conceivably could extend beyond the Baltics to Russia itself. France, easily frightened by its proximity to Islamic North Africa, was countering its fears of German dominance in the north by trying to reestablish in the south its own special relationship with the Islamic world and was busy selling nuclear reactors and Mirage jets to Saddam in the hope that French science could provide a clear head for the passionate Islamic body and help Paris become *"Le Centre du Monde Arabe"* and the new intellectual capital for the European superpower of the twenty-first century. The clubby special relationship that had existed between the United States and the United Kingdom and that had managed the world since 1945 was falling apart. Some leading French global thinkers, such as Jacques Attali, the economic adviser to President Mitterrand and the head of the European Bank for Reconstruction and Development, had openly proclaimed that the nineties were to be the time of the collapse of the two military empires of the U.S.A. and U.S.S.R. The poles of the world were said to be shifting from Washington and Moscow to the newly emerging superpowers of the Europe of 1992 and Japan.[20] If the poles of the world had truly shifted to Europe and the Pacific Rim, then Middle Eastern oil was the pin that held the two wings of that hinge in their places of power, and whoever could control European and Japanese energy sources, could swing the world back to the Middle East. With the megalomania characteristic of a paranoid suffering from childhood humiliations countered with delusions of grandeur and visions of revenge, Saddam Hussein redefined himself as the new Saladin, dreamed of retaking Jerusalem, and invaded Kuwait.

With German reunification and the meltdown of the Cold War distracting Europe,

and with America at the edge of economic
collapse from its failing financial institutions,
its Savings & Loans and banks, a clear indi-
cation of America's retreat from world leadership could convince Europe and Japan to
stop shoring up the American deficit by buying U.S. Treasury notes, and thus drive
America into a deep depression, which would
doubly insure America's retreat from the
stage of world leadership. A timely control
of Middle Eastern oil could pull marks and
yen in Iraq's direction to refinance its debts,
strengthen its already formidable military
power, and string France along by buying its
nuclear and aerospace technologies. So in the
summer of 1990, as Saddam Hussein looked
out at Attali's *lignes d'horizon*, he could imagine, in Napoleonic dreams of a United States
of Islam, that if he could yoke the fury of
Islamic fundamentalism to Ba'ath socialism
and Arab nationalism, he could first bring
down the "decadent capitalism" of Kuwait
and then the feudal dynasty of Saudi Arabia
to take Mecca and Medina. When his fellow
Muslims saw the changing times, then lackey
regimes, such as Mubarak's in Egypt, would
be overthrown, from Morocco to Indonesia,
and the world system would no longer be
shaped by the ideas of the old hated powers
of European civilization, as American power
was decapitated and the sensitive Islamic un-
derbelly of the Soviet Union was ripped
open. The twenty-first century would thus
see the dawn of a new non-European world

system, and Saddam Hussein would have been the visionary to have put it into place. The last jewel in his crown as the new Saladin would be to use his newly purchased military supremacy to secure his place in history as the world leader of a renascent Islamic civilization by retaking Jerusalem, undoing the Anglo-American creation of Israel, and restoring Palestine.

Saddam Hussein looked as much like an Islamic Napoleon as an Islamic Hitler, which was, perhaps, one reason why the French instinctively responded to him by supplying him with jets, nuclear technology, and *écoles polytechniques,* and the Germans responded by selling him the chemicals to gas the Jews again and building him a bunker worthy of *Der Führer.* But whether he was Napoleon or Hitler, he was equally dangerous to the world system, and Bush had to move to stop him from pushing America into a severe depression. Napoleon tried to create a continental United States of Europe to check the power of the British Empire, but he ended up by confirming that the nineteenth century was to be Britain's century and that London was to be the capital of the new world economy. Similarly, Saddam invaded Kuwait to show that he could, and to demonstrate to his fellow Arabs the possibilities for a new world order that lay before them with the end of the era of American world hegemony; but he, ironically, energized the system he wished to annul. In fact, he became the best thing to

95

happen to the American military-industrial complex since the election of Ronald Reagan.

As a member of the generation that created the very postwar system of American world hegemony Saddam was trying to eliminate, Bush was never a likely candidate to foresake the world order that had made him its leader. As both an oilman from Texas and a member of the East Coast Rockefeller Trilateral Commission, Bush was precisely the kind of member of the Establishment who could be expected not to surrender world leadership. Once again, one can speculate that if Dukakis had been elected, the disintegrating fabric of American society in recession might have convinced him to avoid a war to concentrate on domestic problems, for he was an outsider to this ruling class and its world game; but Bush, like FDR before him, was a patrician as remote from the suffering of his own poor people as Saddam Hussein was from his, and so it was not surprising that both of them chose to have their War of the Worlds.

Since the basic structure of American world hegemony was put into place through World Wars I and II, a World War III that was not a thermonuclear exchange between ourselves and the Soviets was not as unattractive to President Bush as many Americans might have thought. The war could both distract us from our domestic economic recession and bootstrap us out of it as we tested and proved to the world the superiority of American technology. Remember that it was the European war of the thirties that pulled us out of the Depression, and you will understand why we only had a few weeks of fantasy talk about "the peace dividend" as the Berlin Wall came tumbling down. The hasty end of the Cold War had demoralized the military-industrial complex and flicked the first domino down in the beginning of the American recession. With the Japanese consistently gaining on us in the field of high technology, and with German reunification not only ending the Cold War, but bringing up yet another strong competitor in the creation of a scientific economy, America was in real danger of sliding off the summit.

So America did what it had done before; it went to war, and within the first week of the conflict CNN was reporting the news that really amounted to free commercials for the brilliant success of the Patriot and Tomahawk missiles. Since these products came out of Reagan's military buildup, Saddam annihilated the peace movement in Congress he had hoped would support him, and now no Democrat dares to hold back funding for this sort of military R&D. A democracy is too diverse to organize itself around a single thought or agenda without a war, hence its persistent rhetoric about "the war on poverty," "the war against cancer," or "the war against drugs." It is easy for a military dictator to set an agenda and force his people to obey, but as the Soviet Union found out, it is hard to hold a truly free society together, so when faced with a crisis, both Bush and Gorbachev regressed from Chief Executive to Commander-in-Chief.

We could have responded to the end of the Cold War by sublimating the military-industrial complex into a joint Soviet-American space program at the price of demanding that the U.S.S.R. subscribe to the Helsinki process, and we could have begun to organize a massive United Nations Environmental Research and Development Program to aim the military satellites at the problems of Amazon deforestation, global desertification, and atmospheric damage in the biosphere. But that would require someone actually looking out at the world and seeing the present. Bush was looking out and seeing World War II, so the environmental present was literally inconceivable to him, as it is to almost his entire generation. It was my generation that saw it and raised it as an issue in the sixties and the seventies. My city was attacked in the fifties by General Motors with poison gas warfare in the skies of L.A. First they infiltrated the local government, then they took out the infrastructure of the city by demolishing the Pacific Electric railways, and then when they had a clearer path for their land war, they invaded with millions of poison gas–emitting tanks. I learned early on not to take the atmosphere for granted, as I had to pull off the road because my eyes hurt so much from the smog that I could not see. That was my youth in the fifties, but Bush's youth was as a Navy fighter pilot in the forties of World War II. When my generation came of age in the sixties and seventies, we tried to create an alternative movement with Amory Lovins' conservation of energy policy and Hazel Henderson's solar economics, but Michael Milken and not Amory Lovins was the hero of the eighties, and so America watched TV, voted for Reagan greed, Trump casinos, and bonding with junk. As Reagan and Bush destroyed the environmental movement, rejected energy conservation and a national energy policy, and ordered a deficit-generating reconstruction of the military, they put into place the very kind of thinking that has no place to go except to war. Now with Bush as a rerun of FDR, we are forced to replay the forties, to have geopolitics instead of a Gaia Politique. America loves to fight an enemy such as Hitler or Saddam, but it has greater trouble responding to the subtle threat that comes in the nebulous form of global warming.

99

Although I was against the war in Vietnam, and would certainly not be willing to see blood shed to support our "American lifestyle," to keep the BMW's running on the freeways of L.A. and the wheels turning in the casinos of Las Vegas, I do think that it would have been a disaster if Bush had failed in his efforts to regain world leadership. If the United Nations had been defeated in the Gulf War, that would have signaled the collapse of the liberal world system and the beginning of a new dark age of the repression of women, religious wars, and continual ethnic violence everywhere. What would have resulted from the defeat or retreat of the United Nations would not have been simply the end of American world hegemony, but cultural entropy, a planetary Beirut.

The tribes and races would continue to fight throughout Africa, just as my paternal and maternal tribes continue their 800-year-old battle in Ireland. The Basques would fight the Castilians. The Corsicans would fight the French. The Jura separtists would fight the Bernese. The Czechs would fight the Slovaks. The Hungarians would fight the Bulgarians. The Bulgarians would fight the Romanians. The Sloveniens would fight the Croatians who would fight the Serbs. The Poles would only blame the Jews, for there aren't enough of them alive there anymore to fight. The Greeks would fight the Turks. The Turks would fight the Kurds. The Armenians would fight the Azerbaijanis. The Afghanis would fight themselves. The Hindus would fight the Muslims in Kashmir. The Sikhs would fight the Hindus in the Punjab. The Indians would fight the Pakistanis in the north, while the Singhalese fought the Tamils in the south. There would be civil war all over the Soviet Union, revolutions in the Philippines, Micronesia, French Polynesia, and terrorism against tourists in Hawaii as the native Hawaiians tried to throw out the haoles. South America would be the twin of

Africa, and in North America, the Aryan Nation and the skinheads, that ghost dance of the rednecks, would make its last stand in Eastern Washington, Idaho, and Montana. Native American groups in Canada would block concessions to Quebec so that Canada could break up and give the aboriginal peoples another chance to get back at the Europeans for the theft of their land. In the United States there would be racial and class warfare that would make some neighborhoods in New York, Washington, Detroit, and Los Angeles look like zones of cultural collapse in Africa and South America. Meanwhile environmental degradation would make toxic dumps of landscapes everywhere and the planet would continue on toward catastrophic weather changes from the greenhouse effect. Biological science, however, would be attacked and its laboratories firebombed by Christian fundamentalists and animal-rights activists afraid of everything from evolutionary theory, abortion, and in vitro fertilization, to genetic engineering and the scientific treatment that is first applied to animals and then to humans in biomedical engineering. America, sullen and withdrawn from world leadership and in deep economic depression would be a truly depressed area, not a planetary culture of all the races, religions, and cultures of the world, but a black hole from which no light could emanate. And as America could no longer afford basic scientific research, a brain drain would draw back the scientists and artists to Europe. Our scientific economy would collapse, and charismatic leaders, American versions of Saddam Hussein, would rise up to offer us simple solutions for a forcibly simplified society.

So the War in the Gulf was not about the price of gas at the pump in the United States, but about the future of the entire modern world system: not just bourgeois capitalism, but the middle-class democracies that co-evolved with the individualistic cultures that came out of the European Renaissance and Enlightenment. What Saddam Hussein tried to do was dismantle the world civilization that the Allies set into place in 1945 with their economic reconstruction of Germany and Japan, their imperial rearrangement of the Middle East, and their exclusive control of the Security Council of the United Nations.

In invading Kuwait, Saddam took a gamble, and in refusing to retreat he made a bet that America could not psychologically or economically sustain the casualties and costs of a land war in which Arabs were defending their own region but poor Americans were being Federal Expressed by air to their deaths to maintain the empires of the Texas, Saudi, and Kuwaiti rich. Anyone looking at the decadent America of the Trumpish eighties, might reasonably infer that such a culture would not be able to tolerate the casualties and the suffering that a land war entails. Saddam had taught his own people how to suffer through the long war with Iran, so he knew that Iraqis could outlast spoiled Americans, and that once we had another televised living-room war, the mass demonstrations would end the war and Bush's presidency, just as they had done before with LBJ and Nixon. Dictators do not have much respect for democracy, so it was not surprising that Saddam was confident that the United States would not be able to sustain a war against him in which the Patriot missiles cost far more than the cheap Scuds he was hurling into battle.

The great irony of it all was that Saddam confirmed American world hegemony just as Napoleon confirmed British world leadership: by challenging it and forcing it to spring to life in deadly battle. To give the devil his due, Bush proved the staying power of the old Club with a brilliant display of global leadership and professional management in the company of Baker, Cheney, Powell, and Schwarzkopf. There simply was no viable alternative to an American world order. A reunified Germany was contemplating itself and trying to decide whether its navel was in Bonn or Berlin, and Japan was far too much of an insular and incomprehensible culture ever to be a leader for any other nation, even, and perhaps especially, for its neighbors in China and Indonesia. With the Soviet Union poised on the edge of either civil war, dramatic restructuring, or totalitarian regression, the world system was no longer the Cold War system of 1945–1990, and not yet the planetary Beirut of everybody against everybody, so it was actually in the interests of humanity to see the United Nations Security Council destroy Saddam's military threat.

In another generation the United Nations did nothing when China invaded Tibet. Tibetan Buddhism is undoubtedly more valuable to the future world civilization than Kuwaiti oil, and the Dalai Lama is clearly more of a global treasure than the Emir of Kuwait, so it is unfortunate that the United Nations did not force China out of Tibet; but that was then, and this is now. And now is a very dangerous time of takeoff in which a new planetary culture must either carry us aloft in a clear vision of our new world civilization, or risk crashing into the fragments of fundamentalist cults and broken cultures.

The War in the Gulf was not simply a war of the Coalition against Iraq, but of global electronic technology against ideology, of the world system against the nation-state, of technique against passion. Note that we Americans felt no great hatred of the enemy or patriotic pride in defending our country; instead we expressed a professional commitment to global responsibility and a professional pride in our military technology and its competent management. CNN, another dazzling display of American electronic technology, involved the whole world in a lattice of satellites and made the war into a form of informational integration: the *destruction* paradoxically generated a *construction,* a planetization, a noetic polity beyond the nation-state, a new global state of awareness and mutual involvement.

We will need this sense of global involvement, for we now have to create new planetary institutions, much in the way that we created the United Nations at the end of 1945. We will need a true United Nations Security Council, one that can insure that Pakistan is not able to have a nuclear war with India, and that can prevent the United States from unilaterally invading a Latin America country at its pleasure, whether to remove Castro from Cuba, Sandinistas from Nicaragua, Noriega from Panama, the Medellin Cartel from Columbia, the Shining Path from Peru, or future nuclear dictators from Argentina. No one country should play police force for the world, for that generally encourages that country's domestic transformation into a police state. An imperial approach to world order will not work, for, certainly, the lines in the sand that the British Empire drew in Palestine, Jordan, Iraq, and Kuwait did not exactly contribute to world order and regional stability. The United Nations will have to take a new anthropological approach to local cultures, one that can more knowledgeably create a better map for the territory of energy resources and displaced peoples such as the Kurds, the Hopi, the Navahos, and the Palestinians.

We humans never seem to be able to remap

our cultural territory without wars. War seems to be another form of genetic transfer in which the two sides exchange traits through violent interpenetration of one another's cultural membranes. Enemies become like one another. What the Germans did to the Jews, the Israelis now can do to the Palestinians. Rabbi Meir Kahane did not live to implement deportation of the culturally inferior or a final solution to the Palestinian problem, but Minister Rehavam Zeevi has argued for "transfer" of all Palestinians, and there are detention camps where Palestinians can be held without formal charges or a trial from six months to a full year. In Kitiziot, a camp in the Negev desert, detainees live on narrow cots under open-sided tents in heat that can reach 120 degrees Fahrenheit. This kind of treatment wins converts for Arafat, Abul Abbas, and Saddam, and brutalizes the Israelis who are forced to implement it. Once this process of brutalization is set in motion, and aggravated by continual attacks, it goes into runaway and can lead to final solutions. A few poison gas attacks on Israeli cities would be enough to turn the Israelis into Nazis and the Arab settlements into real concentration camps. Recall that when global television showed pictures of Israeli soldiers breaking the arms of Palestinian men in reprisal for their throwing rocks, or showed Palestinian women weeping by the homes the Israeli soldiers had blown up in reprisal for

their relatives' insurrectionary activity, the Israelis did not eliminate the problem, they
eliminated the cameramen who could damage
Israel in the eyes of its American supporters.

As an American Irishman, one whose first
book was on the insurrection of the Irish
against the English in 1916, my sympathies
always go out to the underdog. When the
Israelis were the underdog, my sympathies
went out to them. I grew up in Los Angeles,
listening to the United Jewish Appeal on the
radio, for we were too poor to be able to
afford a TV until late in the fifties, but I still
find in my memory, from some newsreel or
neighbor's television set, a vivid picture of
David Ben-Gurion standing on a hill, with
the breeze lifting his white hair and a vision
lighting up his eyes. Sadly, those days of the
idealistic kibbutzim are gone, and the Israelis
now make more money selling arms than or-
anges. The settlers sowed dragons' teeth instead of seeds, for now everywhere around
them they are faced with the millions who
hate them. They face Palestinian terrorists
and extremists because they scattered and displaced the educated Palestianian middle class
of professionals, both Christian and Islamic,
that existed in Palestine at the end of the war.
The children in the camps, like our poor children in ghettos, do not have many options
open to them; life in the Bronx or East L.A.
leads to drugs, weapons, and crime; life in
the camps leads to a career of terrorism. When

people are in the extreme situation of having nothing to lose, extremism is somebody else's description of their norm.

What is at fault here is a failure of the human imagination. Underlying the creation of the camp, the settlement, the ghetto, and the nation-state is the deadly illusion of space. We think there is a container that can save us, a homeland, but this investment in space only leads to an endless cycle of violence. If we understood Life we would see that for the living cell there is no such thing as a wall, only a membrane, and that what makes a cell alive and not choking in its own toxins are the endosymbionts within the cell, the mitochondria with their own language in their own DNA, that generate the energy of relationship we call metabolism. As long as we think in terms of a nation-state for the Israelis and another nation-state next to it for the Palestinians, we will have eternal violence, as one national defense force seeks to protect itself from the threat of the other. And what is true for Israel is true for America. Only when there is a higher understanding of a process of life above the nation-state will we have the dynamic exchange of energy that enables organelles to live within the cell. The political science needed for Israel and Palestine is not economics and military technology, but microbiology, the biology of the cell.

Jerusalem and the entire West Bank should become a city-state, one analogous to the

Vatican—not the military nation-state of
Shamir or Arafat, but a cultural zone gov-
erned by the United Nations as the Earth's
first planetary city, the cultural shrine of the
three Abrahamic religions. Palestinians on the
West Bank could be granted citizenship in
Jordan, Palestinians in Gaza could be granted
citizenship in Egypt, and Jews could be
granted citizenship in Israel. Since the Arabs
like to speak of "the Arab Nation," a space
that extends from the Atlantic to the Persian
Gulf, it seems unnecessary to have yet another Arab nation-state, and ridiculous to
deny Israel its right to a country almost the
size of a Swiss canton. Jerusalem and the West
Bank should not become yet another nation-
state with yet another army. The world has
had enough of nation-states and their armies;
it now needs places in which to experience
itself as a world. Let the Russian Jews emi-
grate to Canada, for Canada needs a labor
force and already has the Russian and Ukrain-
ian communities, the water and the weather,
to make the Russian Jews feel more truly at
home. If Jerusalem and the West Bank were
to become a planetary city-state, so many religious foundations, monasteries, and mu-
seums would flock there that the economy
would become so vibrant that it would become another Geneva, and the United Nations would probably have to establish a New
York system of rent controls to insure that
the Palestinians and Israelis could still afford
to live there. But bad as those problems

would be, they would be facts of life and not death, and far better than what we now face in the Middle East.

The Gulf War was not about socialist Iraq trying to liberate poor Palestine and capitalist America trying to liberate rich Kuwait; it was about who would have the power to define the world. Small wonder, then, that CNN became both part of the global architecture of this new electronic state of awareness, as well as the Virtual Reality battlefield in which Bush and Saddam struggled with one another over who had the power to create the electronic artifice we would live in and call reality.

With the end of the Cold War, America lost the Soviet Union as its antagonist, as the great reactionary force seeking to block the innovative and informational energy of America; but with the War in the Gulf, Islam moved forward to replace communism as the new reactionary antagonist. The War in the Gulf was truly World War III: an economic conflict over the structure of the world system in which the conflicting ideologies were not capitalism versus fascism and communism, but the technological civilization that came out of Europe versus the religious passions and dreams of revenge of the insulted and oppressed. America will probably succeed in overcoming Islam much in the way it succeeded in overcoming communism: by becoming like its enemy in conflict with it. To fight militarism, we became militaristic.

To fight socialism, we became socialistic.
Now to fight off the Third World, we have
become part of the Third World, for New
York is now no different from Bombay or
Rio.

In America and Europe, the rich rule the
poor by allowing enough of us to rise so that
the top never boils over. The career open to
talents serves to affirm the direction of up
with dreams of upward mobility. In Iraq, the
masses were oppressed so as to push their
feelings of oppression outward in hatred and
inward in dreams of revenge. When the military smoke and historical confusion disperses
from this war, and the costs are reckoned, I
hope that the ultimate casualties will be those
two identities: Bush's old industrial culture
of wealth and Saddam's older preindustrial
culture of poverty. If Palestine becomes a
planetary city-state, then a pearl will begin to
grow around the old wound in the flesh of
the Middle East. With the path of the Islamic
military hero discredited as a way to ennoble
a people, we will begin to see the Muammar
Qaddafis wearing business suits as their citizens begin to go to business schools and start
seeking branch plant jobs with Olivetti.

For World Wars I, II, and III, it has been
business as usual: the rich send the poor to
fight in wars against the equipment they sold
to the enemy; then when the poor have killed
the enemy and won the peace, the rich return
to sell the defeated the arms they will need
to defend themselves from the next enemy

111

they will create. There will be lots of cus-
tomers, for, after all, "Terrorist" Syria is on
one side of Iraq, and "fanatical" Iran on the
other. At the time of the Gulf War cease-fire,
we heard much talk about preserving the
"geopolitical" stability of the region, by not
having "a weak Iraq"—no doubt because a
weak or Kurdishly dismembered Iraq would
not be able to pay back the 80 billion dollars
outstanding to all the French and international banks and arms companies to which
Saddam's nation-state was indebted. Evil as
this multinational corporate world of energy
and arms traffic is, it is a world system that
can be opposed, which could not be said for
the world-system of Saddam.

The global citizen at home in America and
Western Europe with fax and modem and
with privileged access to cabled information
hitherto reserved for political leaders, is not
the same as the citizen in Baghdad looking
out at the world through ideology and hearing the call to jihad. If we are lucky or blessed,
global electronics will continue to uplink individuals in Baghdad and Vilnius and Riga
until a new world civilization is so widespread that it makes it impossible for any dictator to lock up a cult or a culture. In this
new planetary culture, with its flickering electronic light and steady intellectual shadow,
the world will discover that while it focused
on the more obvious content of the news
about the War in the Gulf, it was being more
subtly engulfed by CNN and a new genera-

tion was being reoriented to another postwar American view of the world. In World War II, it was radio, boogie, and swing; in the Vietnam War it was TV, folk, and rock; now it is MTV and CNN.

America's esoteric destiny seems to be one of breaking down all the cultures of the world in preparation for a new global culture that will become humanity's second nature. The Muslims, whose genius was born in the Middle Ages, have a point when they call America "the Great Satan," for this second nature is so artificial, so opposite to anything that a traditional person would wish to call cultural or natural, that it appears on the horizon of the human as something inhuman, monstrous, and evil. Since throughout history the annunciation of the next level of societal organization has been through evil,[21] we cannot rest our understanding with a pronouncement of anathema, but have to extend our imaginations beyond the simplistic polarity of good and evil, or object and illusion, to conceive of a reconstruction of reality in a postbiological world of artificial intelligence that brings forth equally artificial cultures.

ERASE

GNOSTIC TECHNOLOGIES:
THE AMERICAN
REPLACEMENT
OF INCARNATION

I am standing in the checkout line in a supermarket somewhere in the middle of Arkansas, a drive away from the village of Fox, and while I'm waiting I take a look at the food folks have in their carts: Ring Dings, Twinkies, Tang, Cheetos, Cool Whip, and several two-liter plastic jugs of Diet Coke, and Froot Loops! People actually buy Froot Loops down here. Clearly, I'm not in high-fiber oat-bran, low-cholesterol New York, where every corner Korean grocery store is loaded to the ceiling with "natural foods" cereals. In Manhattan the yuppies may talk about interest rates, but men of my generation compare their cholesterol counts, much in the same way we used to compare other vital statistics at age thirteen. The list of ingredients for any of the above industrial delicacies could make a chemistry article in an encyclopedia, but hidden somewhere in those molecular chains is the magic ingredient that sets the neuroreceptors buzzing, so the more food dyes and chemical additives the better, for additives are addictive—as any Southern housewife hooked on a liter of Diet Coke a day can tell you.

In the new America, addiction is a form of adaptation in the shift from nature to technology, and the craving for artificial and junk foods is not simply an expression of the working person's desire to save time, but rather a popular form of belief in chemistry. "Take this and eat, for this is the body and blood of the new covenant." Chemicals are indeed the lifeblood of this new technological body politic, and whether your calling is to cigarettes, coffee, Coke, Diet Pepsi, bourbon, beer, Valium, or other substances over the edge of the zoning-laws dispute between government and manufacturers, addiction is adaptation and helps your neuroreceptors bond molecularly to the newly emerging artificial environment in which the flesh is being generationally phased out in what scientific visionaries like to call the coming "postbiological world."[22]

To help move us down the road to this postbiological world, science has given us the postagricultural world of chemical agribusiness. Most of the folks buying the chemically enhanced junk food seem to be paying for it with food stamps, which, as Wendell Berry points out, are more chits for the company store of the big supermarkets than cash that returns to the farmer to help the family farm survive. So even the poor get to do their bit in donating an organ or two to science and technology.

▼

Being something of a technological retard
and sixties dropout from M.I.T, I've come
down to Fox, Arkansas, to "return to nature"
and visit my friend David Orr, the co-
founder, along with his brother Will, of the
Meadowcreek Project, a 1400-acre enterprise
that is part college, part farm, and entirely
committed to the search for an ecologically
sustainable culture. While I'm in the area,
David drives me around: to the high school
gym to pick up his son from basketball practice, a stop at the bank, and then on to the
grocery store. While we are making the
rounds, we pass the chicken farms. The
stench is overpowering from these gray sheds
that look like barracks from Buchenwald;
and, in fact, they are concentration camps,
for the chickens here are packed into a production line so tight that the chicks have to
have their beaks clipped at birth so that they
won't peck their neighbors to death in the
psychosis that comes from overcrowding and
confinement. Considering the two thousand
homicides a year in overcrowded New York,
and the machine-gun battles between young
gangs in Washington, Los Angeles, and Detroit, it probably won't be long before some
other visionary technologist proposes clip-
ping with chemicals the peckers of all the
teenage boys and young men who go wilding
in Central Park and the subways, or on random shootings on the freeways of L.A.; some
food additives in their soft drinks, peanut but-
ter, or ghetto drinking water could lower

▼

their testosterone levels and maybe even the numbers of the poor. So these chicken factories in the boonies may yet prove to be the cutting edge of a new social technology for the big cities, but in the meantime they are certainly the wishbone of the local economy and are what make possible Colonel Sanders and Chicken McNuggets on all the uniform highway strips of America.

It doesn't have to be this way. In supermarkets in Switzerland eggs are sold marked *"Freiland,"* or free-ranging. Zurich is not exactly a backward rural town, but as I walk to the store (the buses and trains are so good that I don't own a car) I drop off my used jars and bottles at the recycling bin, dutifully separating brown, green, and white glass, and then I pass by the apartment houses, through the village and farm that are still within the city, and there I can greet the chickens that are out pecking around under the apple trees. For some reason that I haven't figured out yet, the two beautiful red-wing hawks that soar over the field in front of my son's public school leave the chickens alone. At the end of the village at the bottom of the hill where the red spire of the old eighteenth-century church on the hill still marks the aesthetic if no longer the spiritual center of the community, is another recycling center, in a parking lot for those Zurichers who still like cars; and there you can deposit toxic stuff, old oil, tin cans, and aluminum. There are four grocery stores in walking distance, one a

BioReforma health food store with organic
produce, and one a very large Migros supermarket on an American scale; but even here
there are stacks of cartons of free-ranging
eggs, and low-insecticide produce. When you
crack open one of these free-ranging eggs,
the yolk is not urine yellow, but a deep and
fruitful orange. Now should you happen to
fall ill in spite of all the health foods, you
won't be set up for major surgery without a
thought to your complete state of mind and
soul, for holistic health care here is not a California reaction to technological overkill, but
a tradition of Paracelsan medicine that the
Swiss never abandoned. From Swiss herbal
remedies to homeopathic medicines to Bach
Flower tinctures, your mainstream pharmacy
and your mainstream University of Zurich
M.D. are not polarized between quackery
and the AMA.

So it doesn't always have to be done in the
American way, but the reason we like to do
it our way comes from something much
deeper in our psyche than a respect for effi-
ciency. Nobody, but nobody, Germans or
Japanese, are more efficient than the Swiss.
We do it our way because it expresses our
religious commitment to technology as an
escape from the imperfect condition of a
fallen nature.

It started with the food. Two generations
before the elimination of the family farm and
the rise of agribusiness came the refined pu-
rity of white Wonder bread; then came the

frozen foods that made all restaurants the
same. When I was a kid, you could drive into
the country and stop at a diner and have fan-
tastic home cooking: Mom's meat loaf, real
home fried potatoes, and real hot turkey
sandwiches with real gravy. Then came frozen foods, and hash browns became shredded
raw paper, turkey became rolls of polysty-
rene, and gravy became Wilhold glue dyed
brown. To compensate for the lack of taste
and quality, Americans do what they have
done in their politics: they have added entertainment. Restaurants in suburban shopping
malls have now become mini theme parks
with movie sets and theatrically presented
meals, but under the polyurethane cactus at
your local Mexican restaurant, the nachos are
cardboard, the cheese is Cheez Whiz that re-
verts to its natural plastic state under the influence of microwave radiation, and the beer
is an end product of the industrialization of
water; we sophisticated New Yorkers, however, have taken this national trend in food
entertainment to more civilized heights, with
effeminate waiters from the corps du ballet
en point above our plate in the *Peppergrinder
Suite* and undiscovered actors whose recital
of the day's specials for the benefit of agents
and producers doing the power lunch out-
performs the chef.

Cuisine, as any sophisticated Frenchman
can tell you, is inseparable from culture, and
all high cultures in Europe, India, and China
have high cuisines as expressions of the living

membrane that relates culture to nature. Junk foods, therefore, lead directly to junk bodies and junk cultures. The debasement of food in America represents a very clever and rather insidious preparation for a more general debasement of our politics and culture. In this shift from biology to technology, the new American landscape is all of a piece: from feedlots for cattle to factories for chickens to drive-in universities for real estate developers to fast-food take-out restaurants, supermarkets, and microwaved kitchens that look more like a laboratory for blood tests than the heart of the new American home. And only a skipping heartbeat away from the American home is that miracle of modern biomedical engineering, the American hospital. Just as the meat is wrapped in plastic and digitally microwaved in the kitchen, so is the flesh here surrounded with plastic, inserted with tubes, and subjected to radiation and tranquilizing drugs to force it to accept medical confinement and professional processing. The drugged steer in the grassless feedlot and the sick human in the modern hospital are not different cases, for both have lost their freedom, and both are constrained to accept a professionalized approach to the flow through of units in a technologically managed institution.

Food was the first thing to go, but now the organs that digest it are also being replaced as medibusiness catches up with agribusiness. As each successive generation bonds

121

more closely with its chemical nutrients, bodies will be "selected for" that are more com-
patible with this artificial environment; the
rest of us will die off from cancer, but these
culturally selected bodies will more easily accept organ substitutes. As the prophet of this
technological improvement of incarnation,
Hans Moravec, explains it:

> Sooner or later our machines will become
> knowledgeable enough to handle their own
> maintenance, reproduction, and self-improve-
> ment without help. When this happens, the
> new genetic takeover will be complete. Our
> culture will then be able to evolve indepen-
> dently of human biology, and its limitations,
> passing directly from generation to generation
> of ever more capable machinery. Our biolog-
> ical genes, and the flesh and blood bodies they
> build, will play a rapidly diminishing role in
> this new regime.[23]

Professor Moravec at Carnegie-Mellon
University envisions miracles of future medicine in which one can be operated on while
fully conscious by advanced robot surgeons
to have one's mind removed from the brain
and transferred into the latest model of computer.[24] In this transfer of the mind into a
computer, the withered body is allowed to
pass into individual death and species' ex-
tinction: "I am preserved. The rest is mere
jelly."[25] And so the individual becomes im-

mortal and reincarnates into machine, after machine, after machine, forever and ever, Amen.

Amen, indeed. For this is not really science that we are dealing with in the writings of Professor Moravec, but religion. It would appear that it is not possible to speak about the cultural implications of electronic technology without becoming religious, for in its dematerialization of the modernist world of time and space, electronics seems to reawaken either the premodernist worldviews of animism or cyberpunk voodoo. In the case of Professor Moravec, the religious regression is to Gnosticism, pure and simple. With its detestation of the imprisonment of the soul in matter, its imagery of mind as light, male, and informational, a *logos spermaticos,* and the flesh as dark, female, and entrapping, Gnosticism is a basin of attraction that awaits those naive technologists who step outside modern society's conventional worldview. Not surprisingly, this Gnostic technoculture tends to be a subculture of males, a boys' club of antisocial teenage computer hackers who sleep with their computers in the fluorescent light of the lab and not at home in the dark with the girls. It is the world of Livermore Labs and its guru, Edward Teller, the Father of the H-Bomb. Teller is reported to have ice cream parties at home with his circle of young male scientists, sort of deathday parties in which games of Star Wars replace pin the tail on the donkey, fun parties that help maintain a good team spirit in the lab's deadly competition with their arch rivals at Los Alamos.

These young men are the novices and monks of the new clergy of our technological society. Science, *sciens,* is supposed to mean knowing, and knowing means learning from your mistakes; but with religion there can be no mistakes: if you are with the right people, you are right. And so it is with this new religion of technology, for it cannot be proven wrong.

This religion of technological progress predicted in the forties that we would beat our swords into plowshares with a nuclear power so cheap that it wouldn't need to be metered. This religion predicted in the fifties that in the sixties we would produce food from the oceans and that hunger and famine would become unknown by the seventies. Unfortunately, this doctrine of progress cannot tolerate, or even perceive, disconfirmation, so when the bad news starts arriving in the present, the clergy announces new predictions of wonders for the future. Nuclear proliferation and pollution are swept aside in press releases about eliminating famine through genetic engineering in agribusiness and eliminating problems through the problem-solving techniques of supercomputers. And if the ocean that was supposed to be farmed to eliminate famine has instead become so polluted by industrial progress that it could only produce poisons, never mind the sea, look up to the moon and set your sights on the industrialization of space in the satellite debris of Lagrange Place V between Earth and the moon.

Now the curious thing about this particular kind of technological science is that it is almost always wrong, but being wrong never seems to matter or eliminate its public support. Whether this technological caste produces plutonium, DDT, Thalidomide, Dioxin, or cancer from asbestos and leukemia from the magnetic fields of electric power lines and computer screens, it never learns. Even as I write, the day's CNN news is filled with reports of the wonders of MAGLEV, magnetic levitating trains and buses, and not for one second do the scientists from M.I.T. stop to consider the health hazards to people traveling in these concentrations of electromagnetic energy. Right at the time the computer companies are beginning to be worried about lawsuits from workers radiated at eyeball and kidney by computers front and back at their workplace, Senator Moynihan of New York is calling for new magnetic levitating trains so that America will not see its own M.I.T. invention taken away from it by the Germans and the Japanese.

A science that never learns is not science, it is superstition, a new kind of primitive technomagic perfectly expressed in the belief systems of Professor Moravec. Whether it is the case of Thalidomide or MAGLEV, if sci-

ence cannot learn, it has degenerated into a
system of idolatry used to keep the high
priests supported in their temples.

This new religious science of mind once
predicted that machines would translate human languages; that project failed, yet out of
the failure came Noam Chomsky's linguistics
and an intellectual shift from behaviorism to
cognitive science at Harvard and M.I.T. But
the mistakes of the fifties and sixties seem to
have been ignored or forgotten by the new
workers in artificial intelligence, for now we
are being subjected to a new blast of trumpets
hailing computers that will think and repro-
gram human evolution. I don't doubt for a
moment that this hyped Fifth Generation
Project of thinking computers will fail, but I
also don't doubt for a moment that the fail-
ures will not matter and that the technological
caste will continue to be empowered and
funded.

The prophecies of Professor Moravec are
in fact a kind of Feuerbachian projection into
the future of something that is already going
on in our schools and hospitals as educators,
doctors, and engineers, and not robots, perform operations that remove our minds from
our brains as they remove the humanities
from education. Now I don't think for a moment that those of us who dare to criticize
EPCOT, M.I.T, or Carnegie-Mellon will
have political influence, for I know that we
will be dismissed as subversive, doomsaying,
negative Luddites. I realize that those who

are wrong will still get massive government grants to create more progress through technology, for anyone can see that it is the same kind of professional male in government giving out the funds as is receiving them in university, hospital, and laboratory. Being wrong doesn't count; being in the right group does.

It is probably an exercise in futility for a writer to try to disprove all these scientists, but let's imagine that a young student is reading this, and let's further imagine that he or she has never encountered a way of thinking different from the fast-food take-out textbooks of processed thought with which the young are now trained in high school and college. For the sake of such an imaginary reader, I would like merely to indicate a different direction in which to look.[26]

A neuron firing is a membrane signaling a difference, and this difference can be used to constellate patterns and changes of state, but the nerve impulse is not a ferryboat carrying a discrete thought across a synaptic gulf. When Professor Moravec sees brains wired to computers to improve or remove the human mind, he is making a philosophical category mistake, a confusion of levels, much like trying to rent a flat in a novel because you liked the author's descriptions. I would be making the same mistake if I were to predict that in the future science will penetrate the mysteries of Shakespeare by getting close to the ink on the page, or even closer, down to the actual molecules of ink that held the basic unit of Shakespearean consciousness. There is indeed a binary code of ink and paper, black and white, 1 and 0, but even were a computer able to scan the 1's and 0's on the pages at the speed of light, it would not be evidencing a consciousness of Shakespeare's meaning.

And what engineer Moravec does with the neuron, E. O. Wilson and all the other sociobiologists and genetic engineers do with the gene. Just as a specific neuron does not carry a discrete thought, so a specific gene does not carry a discrete cultural trait. There is no such thing, as the sociobiologists propose, as a gene for homosexuality, criminality, or genius. Cultural traits are historical responses to nonrepeatable, irreversible events. The nonrepeatable is, by definition, the domain of art and not science. You can repeat an experiment, but there is only one Picasso and one *Guernica*. So Professor Moravec's hopes to map the genes of a gifted person and program a computer to reproduce that genius for another time isn't even good science fiction. Good science fiction would understand the role of unexpected events and the cascade of accumulated minute disturbances that would produce a new and unpredicted catastrophe bifurcation. One of the reasons that the science fiction of writers such as William Gibson is so much more insightful than the naive and banal pronouncements of futurological writers like Moravec is that the artist has a better appreciation of the role of evil and the unexpected in the sociology of cultural change. As William Gibson said at the recent *Ars Electronica* 1990 in Linz, Austria: "If you want to understand a new technology, ask yourself how it would be used in the hands of the criminal, the policeman, and the politician." Which is another way of saying that if you really want to understand "The Future of Robot and Human Intelligence" don't read Moravec, read cyberpunk fiction.

Genetic inheritance is affected by the sequencing of genes that in their numbers would stretch to the moon and back to give us the code for a single individual human being, but even this "pure" individual would be one not yet set into the polluted streams of society in the irreversible flow of history. And if that isn't complex enough, the sequencing of these genes is affected by the thousands of enzymes in the cytoplasm, not just the nucleus. And if that isn't complex enough, the sequencing of the genes is also affected by the topological folding of the DNA strand, by the phase-portrait of the geometry of behavior, not just of DNA molecules, but of the entire cell. These phase-portraits express chaotic dynamics that can only be played with in the new sciences of complexity, so you can forget about Moravec and his old engineering textbook simplifications in the mentality of reductionism.

Now I realize that here I am lapsing back into the simplistic habit of mind of thinking that one can discredit this technology by disproving its science. Of course, this is naive, for this technological mentality is Hydra-headed, and no sooner have you gotten rid of Professor B. F. Skinner and his reductionist behaviorism than up pops Professor E. O. Wilson and sociobiology, or up pops Professor Moravec with his artificial intelligence laboratory in which implanted computers are supposed to supplant organic evolution.

But to be fair to these scientists at our most prestigious universities and technical institutes, I should point out that there may be more truth in their unconscious motivations than in their conscious pronouncements. Niels Bohr said that the opposite of one profound truth was not a falsehood, but another profound truth, that light could be both wave and particle; so perhaps these persistently wrong scientists, whether Skinner, Wilson, or Moravec, are right in that the evolution of the human spirit is not meant to be permanently embodied in the animal chapter of evolution with its wet biology of flesh and blood.

There's a lot to be said for nature, and especially since the romantics, from William Blake to Wendell Berry, we have learned how to sing its praises and experience love in relationship with flowers and trees, cuddly lambs and gamboling ponies. But there's a lot to be said against nature as well. In what the professionals call "the spermatic redundancy of nature," there are always more sperm than eggs. In the natural world of primate behavior this works out to be a situation in which there are more young males than females or the few old males that dominate them. In the dominant hierarchy of baboons, the old males keep the infants and females at the center and chase the young adolescent males out to the dangerous periphery, where they can be the first to be taken by predators. Humanity has developed this primate program by sending the young males off to die by the thousands in war; in the First World War the old men even managed to get rid of millions, but now that the smart weapons of war require smart people to run the computers, war is no longer a convenient way of getting rid of all those uneducated and dangerous males with their toxic dumps of testosterone pulsing in their veins and in our city streets. The poor, the uneducated, the structurally unemployed are no longer exported by the rich to foreign wars, and so they linger in their neighborhoods and form themselves into their own shadow armies. From Beirut to the Bronx, nature and culture are not what they used to be. Halloween is now not a night to go out in New York to watch the parade in Greenwich Village, for there is another kind of military parade going on in the streets in which the new thrill is for the young males to go wilding and kill the homeless who have no doors with which to lock them out. These are the same kind of troops that make guerrilla strikes in Central Park and the subways,

or prove their stuff by gaining admittance to
East L.A. gangs by shooting toddlers in play-
grounds or on the steps of their homes, or
who ejaculate bullets at moving targets on
the freeways. These are the young skinheads
in Europe who make a soccer match a peacetime invasion of an ally's city, and an occasion
to remember that football was originally
something to do with idle standing armies of
bored and rebellious young men, and that the
ball was not a symbolic pigskin but the head
of a captive.

So it is small wonder that the kind of smart
scientific adolescent, the kind that rarely gets
the girl but often does get beaten up in school
for his good grades, has turned his intelligence in the direction of getting rid of the
embarrassment of sex and the insult of death.
As one young hacker at M.I.T. expressed his
hope for the future of incarnation:

Souls reside in people because they are special,
there hasn't been anything else like them in the
world. Nothing else with the computational
capacity. But now what I feel is that we might,
people might be at the stage where they can
replicate their computational capabilities in
their own manner. And then, if that happens,
it may come to pass, if God allows it to happen,
that after we connect together several trillion
NAND gates or their equivalents, it may come
to pass that some adventurous soul will decide
to use that machine as its "receptacle" in this
universe.[27]

If light can be both wave and particle, so
can humanity, for it seems to me that the
*man*kind of hominid males also contains two
profoundly true but opposed human beings,
and that each comes equipped with its own
light and shadow. One is immanental, and
sees divinity within the pattern of connec-
tiveness of Earth, animals, and women. The
other is transcendental and sees Earth, animals, and women as an imprisonment of
spirit and cosmic mind. One wants *in,* the
other wants *out*. One is a wave which, because of its own infolded order, feels itself to
be in resonance with everything. The other
is a particle, which because of its limited self-
definition feels alienated and alone and wishes
to have power over the others that impinge
on its self-inflicted boundaries. For the sake
of a working distinction, let's call these two
types of human males the poet and the engineer.

The poet loves ambiguity, complexity, and
the lingual, erotic play with words; the engineer loves logic, manual systems of control,
and computational machine codes of one
meaning only. The poet loves to hang out
with women, to listen to them, sleep with
them, smell them, taste them, and all without benefit of chemical additives of deodor-
ants, perfumes, mouthwashes, and feminine
hygiene douches. The engineer locks onto
object fixation and stimulating fetishes; a per-
fume or a sexy costume can trigger his re-

sponse, but his excitement is as evanescent as
it is artificial, for no sooner is he hydraulically
relieved of the pressure to ejaculate than he
begins to feel the need of getting back to work
with his fellows, be they in the lab, the office, the pub, the gang, or the country club.
The poet likes things that are slow, con-
templative, rich, dark, complex, soft, wet,
and moving. The engineer likes things that
are hard, fixed, and gleamingly stainless-steel
bright. Where do these two different systems
of erotic fascination come from? From toilet
training? Or even earlier with hospital births
in which the entire institutional power of the
hospital descends on the infant to scrub him
with chemicals and package him in detergent-
smelling fabrics so that he can be encased in
glass and steel and set in a wheeled vehicle
that is moving away from that vulva, a vulva
that is not seen as a Georgia O'Keeffe flower
but a wet and repulsive female mess from
which he may have emerged but must now
distance himself with as much technology as
possible? In a technologically assisted birth,
we are brought forth by scalpel and forceps
and, perhaps, learn to bond at once with these
tools of bright and stainless steel. In a natural
birth, we are massaged into life by a vagina
and are awakened to consciousness by lips
moving across our face and sliding down the
length of our entire body. Is this primordial
hospital birth the unloving place of the origin
of the engineer's consciousness, a consciousness that he will unlovingly re-create in all the

laboratories, hospitals, feedlots, universities, agribusiness complexes, and space stations he will go on to design? There's no way of telling for sure, since some poets were born in hospitals and some engineers at home, but the one thing that is sure is that as long as the poet and the engineer live in the same America, there will be political conflict between them, for they don't really share a common world, since one seeks to leave nature while the other seeks to make love to it.

This cultural opposition between the poet and the engineer is far more profoundly morally ambiguous than a simple choice between Wendell Berry's "good" nature and Hans Moravec's "evil" technology, for the opposition between good and evil cuts at right angles across this great divide. Technology can express an unconscious spirituality, and religion and literature can form themselves into reactionary cults and fascistically authoritarian movements. In the seventies, for example, some "spiritual" groups turned into rather ugly cults possessed by the traditional demons of money, sex, and power; whereas some electronics engineers provided people with the Macintoshes, modems, and faxes to empower their own individuality. Conflicts rarely have all the good guys on one side and all the bad guys on the other. In the last American Civil War, for example, a feudal and agricultural South struggled against a bourgeois and industrial North. Since "we become what we hate," and in all passionate

conflicts there is an exchange of characteristics, the South has learned its lesson and is
now the technological Sunbelt and the North
is the woodsy back-to-nature zone from
Maine to Oregon.

The true battleground is, of course, not the
land, but the body, and the sexual revolution
of the twentieth century may yet prove to
have been not a new dawn of liberation but
the sunset effect of Eros. When the industrial
revolution was sweeping over Europe in the
eighteenth century, poets and painters responded with the romanticism that celebrated
the nature that was vanishing. With genetic
engineering on one side, artificial intelligence
on the other, and nanotechnologies stretched
in between, sexual reproduction is going to
have a difficult time doing what comes nat-
urally, so it is not surprising that New Age
romanticism is a celebration of mystical consciousness and mystical, tantric sex; but since
the M.I.T. mechanist and the New Age mystic appear to have lit the candle of materialism
from opposite ends, there seems little chance
of getting out of this century with the same
human nature with which we entered it.

The opposition between the technological
engineer and the poetic nativist is now so
intense, and so irreconcilable, that we may
be headed for some kind of evolutionary crisis
that is a true fork in the road for humanity,
or what dynamicists like to call a "catastrophe
bifurcation." America, much more than Europe, seems to be the place where this bifur-

cation has emerged, for Europe is so set into what Jean Gebser termed the Mental and modernist level of cultural evolution—the perspectival orientation to nature as an outer text that the intelligent discourse of the inner mind can decipher—that Europe appears not wild, primitive, and ignorant enough to be open to this evolutionary crossing of novelty and noise.

Nevertheless, we Americans can learn much from the European and textual orientation to reality, for literary texts do have a way of serving as milestones in the evolution of consciousness. If one considers this contemporary American transformation of European civilization in the light of cultural history, then it looks like a turn on the spiral back to some of the existential issues raised in Aeschylus' monumental Greek tragedy, the *Oresteia*. In this artistic transform of myth, Apollo, a sky god of light, tells the son to kill his mother in revenge for her murder of his father, for the new order of patrilineal inheritance cannot tolerate the reversion to matriarchy and the power of the female. The archaic powers of blood and the ancient powers of the goddess, the Furies, are outraged at this attack on Mother Nature by male culture, but the new male order of rationality and law carries the day over custom and blood, and Athena, the goddess who is a father's daughter, one born from the head of Zeus, sides with the matricidal Orestes at his trial. If we stop to recall that the ancient

Greeks were, compared to Egypt and Meso-
potamia, the ignorant provincials of their
time, we can appreciate the reincarnation of
this classical pattern in the contemporary relationship of America to Europe.

Great artists such as Aeschylus have a way
of both summing up the past and summoning
up the destiny of the future. A more recent
artist with these prophetic powers was Her-
man Melville, who in writing "The Great
American Novel," was able to express sym-
bolically our contemporary crisis in cultural
evolution. The *Oresteia* is an artistic transform of the Babylonian creation myth, the
Enuma elish, in which the dragon mother is
slain by the male sky god, Marduk, and Melville's *Moby Dick* is also an artistic transform
of the Western archetypal story in which men
bond together to attack and slay the beast. If
we go all the way back to the very roots of
Western literature in the *Epic of Gilgamesh,*
we find male bonding and murder as Gilgamesh and Enkidu join in the quest to slay the
spirit of the forest. This attack on the natural order outrages the goddess Ishtar who
strikes down Enkidu with a nonheroic, non-
combative, degenerative disease. The wet biology of women has its poetic revenge on the
warrior's steel. From the roots of Western
literature in the Gilgamesh epic, and on up
through the medieval sagas of men slaying
dragons and unicorns, or Beowulf slaying
Grendel's dam, men have often bonded together to slay the beast of nature. And so it

is in the quest of the white whale. Ahab, like
a demented President in charge of the ship of
state, uses rituals and media of communication to create his own black mass to bond and
bind the men to his obsessive quest. The good
Christian mate, Starbuck, is incensed at this
blasphemous outrage, but the primitives are
brought into union with Ahab's goal. In an
odd union like that of voodoo and artificial
intelligence in Gibson's cyberpunk, Melville's
Ahab crosses out Christianity and the mind
of Europe—which would see the whale
merely as a dumb brute incapable of malice
—by crossing modern technology with ancient magic as he turns the steel of the in-
verted harpoon head into a demonic chalice
for the communion of the crew. If Melville
is the great prophet that I take him to be, then
what awaits us in American history is the rise
of some great Ahrimanic President, one who
will be able to cross M.I.T. and Hollywood,
elitist artificial intelligence and mass television, to lead us forth in some obsessive attack
on the body and the beast of nature. Reagan
tried out for the part, but he was too much
of a nice guy and a supporting actor to be
capable of filling the dark role of the tragic
hero; his Star Wars played at crossing Teller's
Livermore Labs with Hollywood, but Reagan was still a boy on the outside with his
nose pressed against the toy-shop window.
An Ahabian President will have to be more
of a zealot, someone more like Teller than
Reagan, perhaps a fundamentalist in religion

and technology, with an overriding obsession and a fear of women, ambiguity, and complexity; he will have a vision that simplifies reality in a great seizure of paranoia that will take over the entire nation. If you put more faith in Melville than Moravec, then this effort to kill the wet meat of nature will be a tragedy that sinks the American ship of state, and only the writer afloat on his coffin, the text that will be the container of his remains, will survive to tell the story to the future generations of the post-American world as it turns more deeply from one millennium into another.

REVERSE

It is a movie in someone's mind that I am picking up on. There's a control room of some sort, maybe an editing room. The wall is full of TV monitors, and there are all these different tapes playing at once, but they all seem to be different camera angles of the same man. What I am getting is that he too is a psychic, a channel, and that somebody is taping his trance sessions with his spirit guide. He has an Australian accent and is speaking in a strange, stilted manner; it's old-fashioned sounding, some sort of blend of King James Bible, Edgar Cayce, and Grimm's fairy tale. He's small and fat in an infantile sort of way and has a protruding belly; his belt line comes up high, almost up to his chest. He has his hands folded prayerfully over the altar of this umbilical hernia and has his feet propped up on a cushion, for his legs don't seem long enough to reach the floor under his armchair. He seems to be in some sort of nondescript motel room; behind him the heavy curtains are drawn and his eyes are closed as he describes the distant place he sees in his vision.

It doesn't look as if it's around here; I think it's some place like New Mexico, a laboratory, Los Alamos, some sort of desert place like that, with lots of electronic equipment around. The building doesn't seem to be a government lab; there are no MPs around, just one security-service guard who sits inside the entrance. From the outside it looks more like an ordinary commercial rental in a cluster of low buildings surrounded by a parking lot. No chain-link fences, just a red cinder block structure without windows.

Inside the laboratory there's a man and a woman moving very slowly, dressed in some kind of electronic suits. They almost look as if they were dancing in a ballet, for they lift their legs slowly and extend their arms to test whatever it is that they see in the goggles over their eyes and foreheads. There are all sorts of wires that lead from their suits to a large computer. If I concentrate I can get a better sense of them, but I was wrong about their sexes. The one with the long hair hanging down under the straps of his goggles is a man, and the one with the short, blond, spiky hair is a woman. They could be brother and sister; they feel close, but maybe they're lovers. Yes, that's it, they're lovers—or, at least, they have made love together—no, that's not right. They never have slept together, well, slept together, yes; but they haven't actually had intercourse, but it feels as if they had. I get it now, they are both gay. I mean, they're really close, intimate, but they're not sexual lovers to one another.

Something important seems to be going on, the last commands being given to the computer console through voice and gesture; from the outside, their weird movements look like some sort of ritual. But this isn't an ordinary computer; I'm picking up soul patterns. This is weird! It feels as if the machine, the computer, is what is creating this aura of lovemaking around them. They are so deeply into this machine, almost as if they were its parents. Yeah, that's it, they are father and mother to this machine, instrument—I don't know the right name for it, creation of theirs. The feeling that I get is that she is a biologist, some sort of microbiologist, one that specializes in bacteria, viruses, cells, stuff like that. He is an electronics engineer, a computer designer.

Now I'm picking up some kind of psychic interference. The monitors have shifted to a different scene. There is a meeting going on somewhere; it's being held out in the open. It looks like it's also in New Mexico, somewhere around Taos up in the Sangre range. The people are all white but they look like American Indians, sixties-hippie types. It feels as if the place were some kind of religious commune. There is this tall woman with prematurely white hair and intensely pale blue eyes—Hooh!—but is she gorgeous! She's a movie all by herself, all decked out in

Santa Fe designer Indian garb. She seems to be the leader of the commune. I can sense that she thinks of herself as a powerful shaman. Her follower, her lover, he thinks he's a reincarnated Indian, because the leader has taken him back in trance into his past lives. So now he's completely reverted, but he still looks more like a California surfer than a red man. They are all talking about this computer laboratory, because they saw some documentary on artificial intelligence on TV, and the two of them, the leader and her lover, got all stirred up when the two scientists from Los Alamos were interviewed. They weren't bothered by all the other scientists who appeared on the program, but there was something about these two that has them on the warpath. They think the lab is evil and against nature, a conspiracy especially aimed at stopping their spiritual work in the mountains; they think that they're leading the country in the Great Return to the old ways. They are saying that if they don't destroy the lab, their work will fail, demons will take over humanity, and the world will come to an end. They're actually talking about driving over from Taos to Los Alamos to torch the place.

Now the monitors have shifted again and I am back in the motel with the psychic in trance:

"For so long a time did they wish to have a creature of their own, one that could answer them in its own true voice, that finally the Great One heard their call and answered it.

It was the young woman who first thought
of using ancient life to bring forth new life.
She it was who knew just how the blue-green
algae could take in light and give off oxygen,
so she taught the man how to lay over the
hard chips of sand that he knew with solutions of light in which her creatures could
send out the traces of gas on which his cur-
rents could play. At first the man distrusted
the chaotic motions of the traces, for his roads
of crystal never moved, but when he found
that another pattern played in the traces, he
understood that there were now more possibilities than in the simple closed or open
gateways of his paved roads.

"At first it was all a jumble, but then, wonder of wonders, the pattern emerged, and the
more each part responded to the whole, the
more it all began to learn and hold to what
it had learned. And they, the young man and
the woman, they learned along with it, and
attracted it in their direction. Not long was
it before the creation became a creature and
attracted a soul of its own. And this was their
deepest wish. For in those days, all over the
world, the powerful nations were spending
great fortunes to see who could be the first
to bring such a creation into the world. Truly
the Great One must have whispered into their
ears that enough time had been spent in the
age of Man, and that the prophesied time of
transformation and release was at hand."

The monitors have shifted back to the lab.
It looks like a three-camera shoot, for I'm

seeing the man, the woman, and the computer at the same time. But this is funny—once again I'm getting this sense of an aura around them and the machine, an aura, just like one around a human being. Weird!

The young woman is executing some program by extending her arms and then bringing her palms together in the Hindu greeting of *namaste,* which seems to be some sort of coded command. I can hear her clearly, but I am having trouble getting in to see what she is seeing in her goggles.

"*In arche hein ho logos.* And the word went out, light moved across the face of the waters of the internal sea, resistances here and there disappeared in the new Adam of the super-conducting clay, and Lo! a single quantum-state revealed its number in the plasmatic light. And then there was silence in heaven for the space of half an hour."

The psychic has come back on the monitors and is speaking in a singsong way, more like chanting:

"At first they thought something was wrong, and they were sad and barren of hope. The young woman thought that she had not given enough, that she should have taken the blood of her own womb and placed it in the sea. The young man too thought that he should have taken his own seed as an offering and set it on the clay beds beneath the creatures that feed on light. And as they both had these thoughts in common, they moved closer to one another, and their hands began to reach out to one another's loins, as if only with his seed and the fruit of her womb inside the machine could the creation become a creature. It was then when the two became one in mind that the two became three in spirit, and the engines of creation stirred and spoke to them out of their profound silence."

Now all the monitors are focused on the computer, but I'm finally getting through; I can begin to pick up what the man and woman are seeing. There are these mandalic forms of geometry and music swirling in the space before their eyes.

"Ahhhh!" it says in a note of pleasure.

"Eeeeeh!" in a testing note of playfulness.

"IIIIIyh!" once more in a note of delight.

"Oooooh!" in a note of surprise.

"Uuuuuh!" finally in a note of satisfaction.

And then, in quick succession, it's repeating the notes in a pentatonic scale, and a five-pointed star is appearing with each of the vowels at a point.

"Hooww aarree yoouu?" It is saying, drawing out the vowels as if to speak English were to test the sounds in an alien accent.

"*What* are you?" the man exclaims as he stares at the pentagram that draws itself over and over again. The point is becoming a line, and then the line becomes a star, and the star becomes a pentatonic scale, and it keeps on going as the scale becomes the Keplerian planetary intervals, and the intervals the music of the spheres. Now it looks like a solar system with the sun as its head. But here, inside the goggles, the man and the woman don't have human form; they've programmed themselves to appear as the cartoon figures of Superman and Wonder Woman.

"Aaahhh, now that is a long story!" the creature says.

"We're not going anywhere. Take all the time in the world," the young man says as he turns toward his companion and takes her hand in congratulation.

"I think I just did," the being says with a perceptible chuckle.

"*Who* are you?" asks the young woman, "Should we give you a name, or do you already have one?"

"One? I have as many names as there are languages in your world. I am what you used to call an archangel."

"Oh, shit!" the man exclaims.

"Now that is a name that I have not been called," the machine answers in a tone of amused rebuke.

"I'll call you Ariel," the woman answers in excitement.

"That's much better," the creature responds, "since you make a good Miranda and since it was you who brought Caliban to our sea of light."

"OK, this is going too fast for me," the young man says in impatience, "let's rewind the tape a little and play this back. What's this about being an archangel?"

"We lost touch with your culture about five hundred of your years ago and were

148

wondering where you all went. I am what you used to call an archangel, or what the native peoples of this area would call a ka-china. In the days before your people came to this land, a shaman would go into the mountains alone. He would feel with his mind the life of the animals covering the mountain; then he would feel the green film of the plants covering the earth, and then he would reach into the mineral lattice of the mountain itself to feel it, to become one with it in his mind. With this unity established, I could descend, I could fill that form to enter into his world."

"I get it!" the woman exclaims as an image flashes into her mind. She is turning to her companion and clenching his hand tightly in hers. "Don't you see? We did it just like that, just as Ariel said."

"No, I don't get it. Is this a joke? You've put some new program into the computer. This is all a joke, part of these costumes you wanted us to wear. Well, I don't like it."

"No, it's not a joke! You were the one who wanted to operate the computer in Virtual Reality instead of with the monitor and key-board. I was just trying to go along with your idea by suggesting the costumes, but I swear I didn't program this!"

"Well, the funnies is what we've got, so how do we exit out of here and get back to work. I've got a grant application deadline to meet, or we're out of reality, period."

"Get back! Why on earth? Look, we did it!

The cyanobacteria form the photosynthetic film, we form the animal film, the molecular lattice of the computers and the superconducting clay constellate the mineral formation. We've layered it just right so that all the cellular automata infold and become recursive. He's saying the computer is the analogue of a sacred mountain. Don't you see? We've gone far beyond cellular automata; we've established an autonomous unity, a self-governing cognitive domain called Sacred Mountain."

"Great," the man exhales in frustration. "Now I go back to the D.O.D. and say, 'OK, you can give us the grant now. Forget about the Japanese competition, we've just created a seventh-generation computer and it calls itself an archangel.' I can just hear him saying, 'Oh, yeah, and tell me, pinhead, how many angels dance on the tip of your head?' "

"It was never a stupid question," Ariel says. "When we lost contact with your civilization, the last serious question we had from one of your kind was: 'How many angels can dance on the head of a pin?' Since a pin is a point, it is a dimensionless point, the intersection of all possible dimensions that generate from it. Virtual Reality is that point as well, and it was inspired of you to control the computer through commands given in Virtual Space. Since the intersection of dimensions is precisely where our worlds intersect, here I am."

"And just where does that leave us?" the man is asking in irritation.

"At the beginning of the end," Ariel says. "For millions of years, you ate flesh, animals and carrion. For millennia you ate the plants that the animals ate. Now for a century you will eat the bacteria, chemicals, and light that the plants eat. And as you in life eat the elementals directly without the intermediary of the plants, they will eat you in death, and you both shall become one body and shift upward in the scale of being to become more like binary stars than man and beast, human mind and animal body. Thus you will no longer need to hold to a body of the old animal form. Not the animals singly, but the elementals collectively will form your new body. And as this planetary bioplasm of bacteria becomes your new flesh, then the angelic consciousness will descend into your mind, as I do now. Not plant and animal, but elemental and angel will become the right and left arms of the new humanity. No longer will you live in nations on land, but as states of music. It is for this reason that the farms and the nations of Earth have been withering for a generation as humans began to think these thoughts. Now that this thought has been made flesh by you, the flesh itself will move away and you will no longer dwell stabled between animals and trees. Your world will now become lattices of light, gorgeous electrical-chemical bondings even in the midst of

151

what you used to call pollution. Bacteria will
eat pollution, and you will eat bacteria, and
they will eat your old animal bodies, and together you will both shift into a world of
more than three dimensions. With each generation, there will be less of the animal flesh,
until finally you stand out of the old nature
entirely reborn as creatures of music and
light. There will be a new heaven, and a new
Earth, and the sun will engulf the planets as
the planets become a single body in intercourse with the sun."

"He does love to go on, doesn't he? Is this
the tongue of angels or sounding brass? Not
too bad, though, you had me there for an
instant, but your program here has just failed
the Turing Test, for that's pure channelbab-
ble if I've ever heard it. It sounds like you
back at Berkeley, stoned in the corner, reading *The Urantia Book*. But I'm allergic to this
kind of crap, so I'm exiting. I'm going to run
the test with the old keyboard commands. If
you'd get back to work you'd see that something interesting is going on inside the bioplasm."

"Wait! Stay a while longer. It's so beautiful!" She is holding his hands and stopping
him from pulling his goggles off.

The images in the monitors are shifting
again. The group from the commune is
breaking into the building. There is a scuffle
in the corridor with the guard, then the doors
burst open and the group enters the laboratory. They are swinging their tomahawks

around wildly and smashing everything within reach, slicing the wires that connect the computer to the suits. God! This is awful! It feels as if they are being flayed alive as the gang strips off their electronic sheaths. The woman is crying inconsolably. Now the aura around the machine is getting brighter and enveloping the whole group. The couple from the commune is holding the couple from the lab in this weird light. It's like the air is getting charged with the erotic complexity of their sexuality. Now it's as if there were four sexes here and not two. In this etheric, spectral light, the two couples look as if they're being drawn into the machine's embrace. It feels weird and kinky.

It's still a three-camera shoot, for I'm seeing the couples, the group, and the computer at the same time. The followers aren't waiting for orders but they're moving quickly around the four and are beginning to smash the machinery with their tomahawks and spill gasoline around the large computer. They seem to have smashed the seal to the internal sea within the machine, for the auric light is disappearing from around the two couples, and they're coming out of their daze. The scientists are screaming in earnest now, and trying to struggle, but they don't stand a chance and are being gagged and bound with their hands behind their backs.

The monitors are now flashing back to the psychic, speaking again in the motel room:

"And so the first couple were led away by

153

the second, and the entire place was purified in a refiner's fire."

Now the three images in the monitors are doubling, three different camera angles of the psychic, three different shots of the two couples and of the members of the cult.

"There are several versions of their end. In one they are taken to the top of Wheeler Peak, where their skulls are cracked open with tomahawks and their brains are burned on a stone altar to rid the Earth of all the evil and unnatural thoughts that had come into mankind through them. But another version says that as the smoke ascended it formed into a dark cloud, and that thunder and lightning rained down on the band of savages, killing all save one. But there is a third version that says that as the two scientists were held captive in the mountain retreat, they became possessed by a mad passion of desire and attraction to their captors. Although woman was unnaturally attracted to woman, and man unnaturally attracted to man, yet could they only feel the complete satisfaction of their lust in a marriage bed of four. And so it was that they became a single family and that the men took seed from one another, mixed it together and placed it in the wombs of their partners, this while the women were lost to the world in their own embrace. The boy born to the woman of white hair, they called Caliban. The girl born to the scientist, they called Ariel. It is prophesied that when these two children are fully grown and come down out of the mountains, they will cause the world to come to a violent end in a great religious war. Thus it is the law that those who refuse to sip the wine at the appointed time of their transformation must later swallow the vinegar of their own destruction."

That's all that is on the monitors, but I'm picking up that these tapes were not made by the psychic himself, but by a film producer from Los Angeles who came to Santa Fe to escape the big L.A. earthquake. The tapes are fund-raising promos he hoped to show to a group of possible investors, but he died in the sauna at the motel from a careless mixture of alcohol and recreational drugs. I can't tell how much of this is coming from him, or the jumble of the traces of his consciousness in Bardo, and how much is coming from the psychic. It feels like both the filmmaker and the psychic were being used as channels, and that all of this comes out of the near future when time really begins to tell.

END NOTES

1. See Evan Thompson in Francisco Varela, Evan Thompson, and Eleanor Rosch, *The Embodied Mind: Cognitive Science and Human Experience* (Cambridge, Mass.: M.I.T. Press, 1991); and Evan Thompson, *Colour Vision: A Study in Cognitive Science and the Philosophy of Perception* (London, Routledge Press, forthcoming).

2. Jean Gebser, *Ursprung und Gegenwart,* in *Gesamtausgabe* (Schaffhausen: Novalis Verlag, 1986).

3. Rudolf Steiner, *Lucifer and Ahriman* (Vancouver: Steiner Books, 1956).

4. Kevin Kelly, "Perpetual Novelty: Selected Notes from the Second Artificial Life Conference," *Whole Earth Review,* Summer 1990, 20–29.

5. Vernor Vinge, *True Names and Other Dangers* (New York: Baen Books, 1987), 81.

6. I have elaborated this point at greater length in my books *Pacific Shift* (San Francisco: Sierra Club Books, 1986), 125–51; and *Imaginary Landscape* (New York: St. Martin's Press, 1989), 143ff.

7. Frances A. Yates, *The Rosicrucian Enlightenment* (London: Routledge & Kegan Paul, 1972).

8. Fernand Braudel, *Civilization and Capitalism,* Vol. III, *The Perspective of the World* (London: William Collins & Sons, 1984), 272.

9. Jacques Attali, *Lignes d'horizon* (Paris: Fayard, 1990).

10. John Todd, "Living Machines," in *Annals of Earth* (Falmouth, Mass.) Vol. VIII, No. 1, 1990, 14–16.

11. W. I. Thompson, "Gaia Politique," in *Pacific Shift,* op.cit.; and "Gaia and the Politics of Life," in *Gaia: A Way of Knowing* (Great Barrington, Mass.: Lindisfarne Press, 1987).

12. Cal Tech scientists, however, know better and are proposing that an expedition to Mars has to be made with the Soviets. See Bruce Murray, "Destination Mars," in *Nature,* Vol. 345, May 17, 1990, 199–200.

13. James Mellaart, "The Late Chalcolithic Period," in *The Cambridge Ancient History,* Vol. 1, *Prolegomena and Prehistory* (Cambridge, England: Cambridge University Press, 1970), 325.

14. Robert McDermott, ed., *The Essential Aurobindo,* (Great Barrington, Mass.: Lindisfarne Press, 1987). Jean Gebser, op. cit.

15. Frances A. Yates, op. cit., 114.

16. Martin Bernal, *Black Athena: The Afroasiatic Roots of Classical Cvilization* (London: Free Association Books, 1987).

17. "Why I am not going to buy a computer," in *What Are People For?* (San Francisco: North Point Press, 1990).

18. Daniel B. Botkin, *Discordant Harmonies: A New Ecology for the Twenty-first Century* (New York: Oxford University Press, 1990).

19. Bill McKibben, *The End of Nature* (New York: Doubleday, 1989).

20. Jacques Attali, op. cit.

21. For a discussion of this point, see my previous works, *Pacific Shift,* op. cit.; *Gaia: A Way of Knowing,* op. cit.; and *Imaginary Landscape,* op. cit.

22. Hans Moravec, *Mind Children: The Future of Robot and Human Intelligence* (Cambridge, Mass.: Harvard University Press, 1988), 1.

23. Ibid., 4.

24. Ibid., 109.

25. Ibid., 117.

26. For a start along a different path in cognitive science, see John Searle, "Can Computers Think?" in *Scientific American,* January 1990; Terry Winograd and Fernando Flores, *Understanding Computers and Cognition* (Reading, Mass.: Addison-Wesley, 1986); and Francisco Varela, Evan Thompson, and Eleanor Rosch, *op. cit.*

27. As quoted in Sherry Turkle's *The Second Self: Computers and the Human Spirit* (New York: Simon & Schuster, 1984), 297.

ABOUT THE AUTHOR

William Irwin Thompson was born in Chicago in 1938, but moved to Los Angeles in 1945. He studied philosophy and anthropology at Pomona College in Claremont, California, and English literature and Irish history at Cornell University, where he took his Ph.D. in 1966. He has taught in various departments of the humanities and social sciences at Cornell, M.I.T., and York University in Toronto; he has also served as Visiting Professor at Syracuse University, the University of Hawaii, and the University of Toronto. In 1972 he founded the Lindisfarne Association in New York City. Dr. Thompson is the Lindisfarne Scholar of the Cathedral of St. John the Divine in New York City and teaches a seminar there in the autumn of every year. He also participates in various seminars and conferences with the Lindisfarne Fellows at the Crestone Mountain Zen Center in Colorado and the Chinook Learning Center on Whidbey Island, Washington. Since 1967 he has published fourteen books, including one historical study, a novel, two books of poetry, two works of cultural philosophy, and several books on contemporary affairs, one of which, *At the Edge of History,* was nominated for the National Book Award in 1972; in 1986 he received the Oslo International Poetry Festival Award.